loaded

Greatest Ever ENGLISHMEN

loaded

Greatest Ever
ENGLISHMEN

ARCTURUS

Contents

Greatest Ever ENGLISHMEN

Arcturus Publishing Ltd
26/27 Bickels Yard
151–153 Bermondsey Street
London SE1 3HA

Published in association with

foulsham
W. Foulsham & Co. Ltd,
The Publishing House, Bennetts Close,
Cippenham, Slough, Berkshire SL1 5AP
England

ISBN 0-572-02964-0

British Library Cataloguing-in-Publication Data: a
catalogue record for this book is available from the
British Library

Copyright © IPC Media, 2004
Loaded ® is a registered IPC Media trademark

All rights reserved

The Copyright Act prohibits (subject to certain very
limited exceptions) the making of copies of any
copyright work or of a substantial part of such a
work, including the making of copies by
photocopying or similar process. Written
permission to make a copy or copies must
therefore normally be obtained from the publisher

in advance. It is advisable also to consult the
publisher if in any doubt as to the legality of any
copying which is to be undertaken.

Book design by Alex Ingr
Printed in Poland

All text copyright © IPC Media except:
All text by Jon Wilde © Jon Wilde
All text by Pete May © Pete May
All text by Bill Borrows © Bill Borrows
Trevor & Simon text © Phil Robinson

Image copyright notices:
© Topham Picturepoint: pages 10, 11, 12, 14, 16, 17,

19 (top), 20, 21, 24, 25, 27, 30, 31, 34, 35, 37, 38,
39, 41, 42, 43, 44, 45, 47, 48, 49, 50, 52, 53, 56, 57
(top), 62, 63, 64, 68 (top), 69, 72, 73 (top and
bottom), 74, 75 (top), 76, 80, 81, 82, 83 (inset),
102-103, 108 (bottom), 108-109, 120, 121, 124, 126,
127 (top and bottom), 134, 135 (top), 137 (top),
138, 139, 142, 144, 145, 149, 150, 151, 153, 154, 155,
156, 157, 159

© Rex Features Ltd: pages 8, 9, 13, 15, 18, 19
(bottom), 22, 26, 32, 33, 46, 51, 54, 55, 58, 59, 60,
61, 68 (bottom), 70, 71 (bottom), 75 (bottom), 77
(bottom), 79 (bottom), 83, 95, 101, 118-119, 137
(top), 138, 140, 141, 143, 148, 158

© BBC: pages 36, 65, 78, 79, 84, 92, 93, 94, 104,

105, 114, 115, 116, 117, 122, 123, 128, 129, 152

© Hulton Archive: pages 2, 23, 40, 57 (centre), 71
(top), 90, 125, 134, 135 (bottom)

© British Film Institute: pages 88, 89, 98, 99

© The Advertising Archives: pages 91, 112, 113 (top
and bottom)

© Conrad and Gual: pages 110-111

© Fremantle Media: pages 96, 97 (top and
bottom), 100

© Hanna Barbera: pages 106-107 (image an
interpretation by Steve Flight of a Hanna Barbera
original)

Rock Stars

Big Mouths

Foreword

AS THE GREAT SHAUN RYDER once said, "Don't talk to me about heroes, most of these men seem like serfs." When **Loaded** decided, in its very first issue, to devote a page each month to its own heroes, it was quickly established that the award of Greatest Living Englishman could never be just another trophy in the cabinet of sporting heroes, acting legends or history-makers whose achievements were measured on somebody else's terms.

Loaded's heroes were going to be the kind of ordinary Joes whose heroism lay in their particular take on Englishness, their cocked-hat eccentricity or ability to raise hell as only a true son of Albion could.

Thus the very first Greatest Living Englishman was a humble barman. Dave from the Winchester Club in *Minder*, to be exact. His achievement? Nothing more – or less – than having the "gentle heart of the rough-diamond geezer, the avuncular, mum's-the-word, indulgent, heart-breaking NEVERLETANOLDMATEDOWN loyalty of the genial pub uncle, the True Mate." It mattered not a jot that Dave wasn't real. He'd been there, larger than life and brilliantly scripted throughout our formative years – a role model for our future adulthoods; a great example to us all.

And so it went. Over the coming years, comedy greats like Sid James, Peter Cook and Ernie Wise were perhaps more obvious recipients for the award, as were true characters and flawed geniuses like Cloughie, Morrissey or Jeffrey Bernard. Fictional great Englishmen abounded, of course – David Brent, Sweep, The Major from *Fawlty Towers* and Trigger from *Only Fools And Horses*. Even Jesus got a look in (yes, of course he was English. From Macclesfield, apparently), as did Beryl Reid (Greatest Living Englishwoman) and Britt Ekland (Greatest Living Foreigner). But never once did we state the bleedin' obvious. If we chose to applaud a rock star, it'd be the likes of the seemingly least rock 'n' roll Rolling Stone: drummer Charlie Watts. And what magazine would have the skewed genius aforethought to dedicate an entire page to a celebration of the newspaper vendor? Loaded, that's who.

As the greatest ever men's mag continues to celebrate everything that is great about being from Blighty, Loaded would, in truth, be lost without its heroes. The men who inspired us from day one to create a magazine full of great stuff about ladies, great moments in life and generally acting the goat. These are our Greatest Ever Englishmen, reproduced exactly as they originally ran in Loaded. And, living or sadly no longer with us, we'd like you to join us in once again raising a glass of the good stuff. Cheers.

Chris Burke
Associate Editor
Loaded

Presenters

Frank Bough

September 2001

"I AM NOT A VERY IMPORTANT person. I am not a member of the royal family. I am not a politician. I am just a journalist, just a hack TV presenter."
– Frank Bough, 1992.

As you grow up, you make shattering discoveries. Santa isn't real, your parents have sex, Auntie Rowena used to be Uncle Roy, that sort of stuff. Nothing prepared my generation, however, for that fateful day in 1988 when we opened our papers to discover Frank Bough had snorted cocaine with prostitutes at a string of sex parties.

Up until then, when we thought of Frank Bough, we thought of his sports casual jumpers, encyclopaedic knowledge of the Olympic Games and rock solid TV presentation skills. His genial persona enhanced and guided our lives. Middle England was appalled. Others applauded. The 55-year-old was clearly still dangerous.

Frances Joseph Bough's first taste of broadcasting came in the 1950s while he was doing national service in Germany. His football skills noted, he was asked to do a couple

The only recent sightings have been a one off appearance on *Shooting Stars* and a *Grandstand* 40th anniversary special.

of sports broadcasts on the forces radio network. By 1962 he was hosting north-east regional show *Home At Six*. By the end of the decade he'd replaced David Coleman as anchorman of *Grandstand*.

Des Lynam, Johnny Vaughan and any other presenter worth his salt today

acknowledges a debt to Frank. He understood what the people wanted and gave it to them efficiently. "It's not my job to get in the viewer's way," he observed. "I give them the basic facts, then shut up while they enjoy the match they switched on to see." Please take note, Sky Sports.

Bough clocked up 850 editions of *Grandstand*, 14 FA Cup Finals and three World Cups, and also presented *Nationwide*, the BBC's early evening magazine show. When *Breakfast Time* appeared in 1983 he was the ideal man for the job. Just before he started, Frank gave an interview revealing the uncompromising drive behind his success. "I have a golden rule that I never drink before I appear on the telly. When I start in the new job, evening drinking will be ruled out."

And then we got wind of what he was doing instead. "I

Nothing prepared my generation for that fateful day in 1988 when we opened our papers to discover Frank Bough had snorted cocaine with prostitutes at a string of sex parties.

was introduced to cocaine by a woman who I later discovered was a prostitute," he told the *News Of The World*. "During the evening she encouraged me to sniff this white substance which she told me would make me feel better. It certainly did. I'd never felt so relaxed. Later she invited me to have sex with her. But cocaine totally killed my sexual ability – I suppose because when you take it all the blood rushes straight to your head, so it can't rush anywhere else. I can remember seeing three girls and a man fondling one another. There was no question of me joining in."

It took Frank, who left the BBC in 1989, several years to recover from this incident. But in 1992, shortly after he bounced back to front ITV's Rugby World Cup coverage, a fresh set of sexual allegations appeared. More lurid headlines, this time about his visits to a sado-masochistic sex parlour for liaisons with a rubber clad 'Miss Whiplash'. His wife Nesta continued to stand by her man, stating: "I'm not going to be beaten by this, that's for sure."

So what became of Boughy? Caravan in Cleethorpes? Maisonette in Bogota? Nobody quite knows. The only recent sightings have been a one-off appearance on *Shooting Stars* and a *Grandstand* 40th anniversary special. Not enough for a nation that still holds a candle for him. It's one more shattering truth we've learnt to live with as we gaze unfulfilled at Eamonn Holmes in the morning or Steve Ryder of a Saturday afternoon: no one does it quite like Frank.
Chas Newkey-Burden

David Dickinson

February 2002

S OCIETY USED TO respect its elders. Old men of the community were placed on a higher spiritual plane and decorated with stuff, and handed women in payment for their wisdom. These days we just stick them in overheated bungalows and wheel them out for Christmas. Still, every now and again a crafty old codger crawls out of the woodwork to claim the glory he deserves. Such as David Dickinson, aged 59, host of BBC1's smashing *Bargain Hunt* (weekday mornings, at 11.30).

Bunk off work and watch *Bargain Hunt*. Not for the spectacle of watching two competing teams buying and auctioning

Sadly, in 1961 some rather creative book-keeping led to a four-year stretch in Strangeways for fraud. 'I was a young bloke trying to get on. But I took the wrong turning and paid the price.'

tat (although watching some matron from Chatham making £15 on a pair of porcelain peacocks can be strangely compulsive) – no, watch it for Dave. Tobacco permatanned, with a proud badger bouffant, he dominates like a mutant hybrid of Arthur Daley and some check-clothed thing out of *The Wind In The Willows*. The man's got pinstripes, gold and a Regency mourning ring with a rose-cut diamond. He is, put simply, a genuine old-school charmer.

This Morning has already fallen foul of

Bargain Hunt's booming ratings since he muscled in on the post-Richard & Judy fallout and two appreciation societies are 'live' online debating the merits of Dave's attire.

Cheshire-born Dickinson has spent most of his life buying and selling junk: elephant-foot umbrella stands, rusty mantraps and the like. He was quite the player during the '60s, with the E-type,

Tobacco permatanned, with a proud badger bouffant, he dominates like a mutant hybrid of Arthur Daley and some check-clothed thing out of *The Wind In The Willows*.

barn conversion and a thriving mail order business. Sadly, in 1961 some rather creative book-keeping led to a four-year stretch in Strangeways for fraud. "I was a young bloke trying to get on. But I took the wrong turning and paid the price."

It's been a life on the straight and narrow as a self-employed purveyor of 'nicky-nackies' since his release in 1965, until a chance encounter with a BBC producer at a barbecue in the early '90s. "God, you're a real-life Lovejoy!" squealed the excited producer as figures spiralled through his ruthless mind. And so a marriage was born. Four series in, and still David Dickinson may be the only man in the country who could interest you in an Admiral Fitzroy boxy barometer. Nice.
Andrew Woods

Dusty Bin

June 1998

"W E'LL SHOW YOU six sketches and six rhyming clues/Six things to remind you, or perhaps to confuse/All yours to consider, and then to realise/Which clues to reject in your search for a prize." – Ted Rogers, 1979.

At the height of *3-2-1*'s reign as TV's top game show, it was watched by 13 million people every week. Do you think all those people tuned in to watch Ted Rogers remedially spell out the legendarily tedious rhyming clues? Or tap their cumbersome club feet to the sound of wannabe Joe Longthornes banging out 'Mandy'? No.

They tuned in for that moment when Gary and Jean from Doncaster made the mistake of picking the bin. When, instead of winning a brand spanking new bathroom suite containing more plastic than all the false legs in Sarajevo, these two people, who hadn't won anything else in life except each other – would go home with nothing more than a small comedy ornament.

At the show's peak, one and a half million Dusty Bin money boxes were sold. In 1984, one young couple even made the

It took over 1,000 years to establish Christianity as a major force in England, but only two weeks to make the entire country fall in love with a dustbin.

national papers when they were refused a new council flat unless they promised to stick a miniature Dusty on their mantelpiece. When I was 11 years old, I refused to go to school unless my parents dressed me as a bin.

3-2-1 was spawned in May 1978 after Yorkshire TV's head of light entertainment was bowled over by Spanish TV's top quiz extravaganza: the 80-minute *Un-Dos-Tres*. Great Britain was soon gripped by dustbin fever. It took over 1,000 years to establish Christianity as a major force in England, but only two weeks to make the entire

country fall in love with a dustbin.

Only a year into its run, *3-2-1* had polarised the nation. There were the 13 million who watched it slavishly, and the 14 TV critics who believed it to be some kind of ITV/Nazi conspiracy that sucked the joy out of people's heads, leaving them with overpowering hope cancer. If you believed what you read, most of the street crime and rioting that occurred at the start of the '80s had very little to do with Thatcher and everything to do with Ted Rogers threatening to give away free kitchens, obscured behind a smokescreen of misleading and improbable clues. In 1979, the *Daily Express*'s TV critic flipped: "We live in a period rich in deadly television game shows, but there is none which plumbs the depths of witless idiocy like *3-2-1*." Anyone with any sense knew this assault was aimed at Rogers.

Your *3-2-1* connoisseur understood the appeal of the bin. Dusty was an unlikely hero – looking like some pint-sized

He couldn't play Spike Island or write songs about smack and shagging people from behind – he was just a little bin who wanted to make people laugh.

disabled drunk, permanently questioning the insanity and gaudiness that surrounded him, his arms set in a Jesus Christ pose, eating up the pain before it could destroy us. He was the people's star, the Prince of Hearts. He was there for us. He'd often perform wearing some manner of disguise – usually designed to fit the theme of the show. In the early years he'd have to be pushed onto the set by a couple of dollies (often Mirielle or Gail Playfair). He'd come on dressed up as Shakespeare, a town crier or, once, Labour leader Michael Foot. Soon many believed the bin to possess a life of his own, far beyond that of a booby prize. He became a symbol of disappointment. But in Thatcherite England he stood for us all; everybody who had a humiliating job, had to wear a stupid uniform or was forced to pander to the whims of greed and commercialism.

In 1980 Metal Mickey got his own show, and forced Dusty's management onto the back foot. He needed a revamp. With television being overrun by the Oxbridge mafia, Dusty needed to be more 'now', more street, more state of the art. With K9 yapping at the heels of Dr Who, and Buck Rogers' boy/fag Twiki taking the

robotised mascot world by storm, there was immense pressure on Yorkshire TV to make Dusty the stuff of sci-fi future. Boffins were rung up, and Dusty was fitted with 15 microchips, 73 microprocessors and a radio control unit. In short, he was given the gift of thought and mobility. Soon he was dancing, bringing trays of drinks and waving. In showbiz terms he was almost capable enough to marry Bruce Forsyth.

The whole refit cost £10,500 – five times more than the cars that they were giving away on the show back in 1978. His new motor shoes meant that the highways and byways that once had been the stuff of his dreams were now open to him. Promotional tours followed, and with the addition of further mechanisation he was soon able to chop through ribbons at fetes. By 1986, not only could he tap dance like Lionel Blair, but he also seemed possessed of an animal sexual magnetism. Where his belly once contained chip wrappers and hedgehogs,

it now swilled with champagne. He was mixing with the decade's showbiz elite, being photographed with the likes of Tarby, Davro and Princess Margaret.

As American astronauts painstakingly assembled space stations and created re-usable moon machines, we'd managed to make a bin juggle. And for a lot less money. He could play the piano, fly around the studio sporting a 007-style jetpack, escape from Houdini-style chains and ride a bike. He even drove a tank into the studio and bombed the audience with confetti.

More importantly, his success led to feuding with Rogers, who was jealous of Dusty's rapport with the young folk. "It's lucky he can't crack gags," Rogers said to a journalist. "Besides, who ever heard of a dustbin with a heart?"

The final insult came in 1986, when Rogers tried disastrously to undermine Dusty by bringing in another robot, a toy terrier called Garbage the Dog. At their first recording together, Garbage came on masquerading as a bull, with Dusty waiting centre stage dressed as a matador. Dusty was supposed to frighten Garbage by shooting at him with a blunderbuss. Dramatically, the cumbersome weapon got caught in Dusty's cloak, misfiring. Garbage was shot in the head, knocking his eyes out and setting his fur on fire. You could see the pleasure on Dusty's face. The setback was too much for Rogers, who moaned: "It's too time-consuming. I want to be known as something more than the compere of the Dusty Bin quiz."

When the show was finally binned in 1987, it proved to be the end for both Ted and Dusty – who now sleeps standing up in Rogers' front room. His gadgetry couldn't compete for the attention of Britain's youth against the rise of the Happy Mondays and acid house. Dusty couldn't play Spike Island or write songs about smack and shagging people from behind – he was just a little bin who wanted to make people laugh.

The star of ITV's biggest game show was cruelly, unfashionably, ironically back on the rubbish tip.
Phil Robinson

Stuart Hall

December 1994

STUART HALL'S LAUGH is one of the seven great wonders of the world. It is a laugh that suggests a roomful of hyenas set ablaze. A laugh full of anarchy, giddy banality and unbridled *joie de vivre*. A laugh with all the impact of a hard wire brush up the jacksie and a smack in the eye with a wet boot-lace. It's the loudest, longest, looniest laugh in showbusiness and it has served its owner well over the course of his last 30 brilliant, barmy years.

A former racing driver and midfield terrier for Crystal Palace, Stuart Hall began his television career in the mid '60s, presenting the early evening news from Manchester. From the start, it was clear that he was in a different league altogether from the ponderous, poker-faced presenters that cluttered the TV schedules. Hall read the nightly news with the clamorous urgency and off-kilter intensity of a man who had a timebomb ticking inside his Y-fronts. He brought an edge of frenzy to the most humdrum news report: the everyday story of a kitten stuck up a tree in Chesterfield would be delivered with the kind of tumultuous excitement usually reserved for the outbreak of nuclear war. Any vaguely comical news story would be enough to ignite that famous laugh and reduce Hall to a steaming puddle of tearful mirth.

Pretty soon it was apparent that Hall's supernatural energies demanded a less constrained environment than that of early evening news reporting. Launched in the late '60s, the numbskull Olympics of *It's A Knockout* (and its international equivalent *Jeux Sans Frontieres*) would become Hall's natural home for close to 15 years. Each week, have-a-go residents of small-time towns would gleefully compete against each other by dressing

up as ostriches or donning giant carnival heads and clambering up and down greasy poles, cheered on by crowds who appeared to have been let loose from the local loony bin for the evening. One might have been forgiven for assuming that the resident team of presenters were also AWOL from some high security mental institution. There was the ageing Arthur Ellis who refereed proceedings with gunboat diplomacy and constantly dribbled on his shirt. There was Eddie Waring who would lift his trilby and warble incomprehensibly whilst looking after the mini-marathon. But, acting as the show's ringmaster, Stuart Hall was clearly out on his own, urging on the contestants to greater and greater heights of achievement until he was fit to spontaneously combust.

It was Hall's relentless bonhomie and madcap giggling that made the show such compulsive viewing. "Can the giant guinea pigs from Grimsby turn the tables on Gosport?" he would yodel with orgasmic intensity. A master of the post-match interview, Hall would collar a

Hall read the nightly news with the clamorous urgency and off-kilter intensity of a man who had a timebomb ticking inside his Y-fronts.

breathless, red-faced granny in a chicken outfit and yell in her ear: "Fifty eight points! A *Knockout* record!! What's it feel like to make history?" Hall's laughter was epileptic and never-ending, even when gashing his leg falling from a trampoline in Bognor Regis or twisting his testicles whilst dyke-vaulting in Antwerp.

Knockout ran until 1982, after which time Hall concentrated his formidable energies on football commentaries for Radio Two and, later, Radio Five. It was here that he proved beyond all reasonable doubt that he was more than

a few vouchers short of a pop-up toaster. Decorating his commentaries with colourful classic quotations (Shakespeare and Homer were particular favourites), he would rampage through a match like a man possessed. With his voice climbing like a fart in a bath and his laughter scaling new heights of preposterousness, he would manage to make a throw-in on the halfway line during a Wrexham v Workington reserve match sound as exciting as a last minute penalty in a World Cup final.

Shortly after being "let go" by the BBC in the early '90s (the powers-that-be having decided that his style was too jocular), Hall suffered a few setbacks, most notably being charged with shoplifting sausages and coffee worth about three quid from his local Safeway. Complete acquittal followed but his career undoubtedly suffered. Now 64, he lives in a Spanish villa in Cheshire with his

wife, Hazel, and his impressive collection of antique clocks. Persistent rumours that the BBC are to bring *It's A Knockout* back to our screens threaten to return Hall to centre stage where he truly belongs.

"I'm a wild man," says Hall. "A total maverick. A complete one-off. Surely there's space for just one like me on the telly these days?" Few right-minded people would disagree. TV presenters come and go in a fog of anonymity but, as sure as all blimey, only the great Stuart Hall lives out Jack Kerouac's famous dictum that the only people who count are the mad ones, the ones who are mad to talk, mad to be saved, desirous of everything at the same time, the ones who never yawn or say a commonplace thing, but burn, burn, burn like fabulous yellow Roman candles. Stuart Hall: top bloke.

Jon Wilde

Tony Hart

December 1999

DON'T BE FOOLED by the soppy voice and the cravat. Tony Hart is as hard as nails. He's decapitated goats while serving with the Gurkhas on India's North West Frontier, and he's taken on Rolf 'Grizzly Bear' Harris in the battle for supremacy of art-based kids' TV.

And all this despite going to a choir school, working as a window dresser in a ladies' clothes shop and saying the word 'lovely' a lot. Tony may be camper than a tablecloth, but remember – this was the '70s and that was the way to get the ladies then.

He first strolled cheerfully into the world of television nearly 50 years ago. His big break came via the classic, almost clichéd route of a sketch on a napkin during lunch with a BBC executive. It was only a picture of a fish, but it was good

Ah, Mr Bennett. Here, to my innocent mind, was the greatest forbidden love since Oscar Wilde set eyes on Lord Alfred Douglas.

enough to get his dainty foot in the door.

After designing the original *Blue Peter* ship – a pretty impressive claim to fame in itself – Tony found worldwide celebrity in 1964 with *Vision On*. This was a show for deaf children, but even two-eared kids were soon gobbling down the young presenter's cocktail of joviality and creative brilliance in 60 countries.

The '70s brought *Take Hart*, which won

him a BAFTA and, even more prestigious, Most Popular TV Personality two years running on *Multi-Coloured Swap Shop*.

In the '80s it was *Hart Beat*, and by now the format was familiar to two out of three children in Britain: wonderfully inventive pictures, created out of old sea shells and bits of bark before your very eyes; a short comic slot from Plasticine pest Morph (originally call 'The Morph'); and the Gallery, an unmissable parade of wretched splatterings sent in by viewers and selected at random by a gang of lonely pensioners.

And then there was Mr Bennett. Ah, Mr Bennett. Here, to my innocent mind, was the greatest forbidden love since Oscar

Tony may be camper than a tablecloth, but remember – this was the '70s and that was the way to get the ladies then.

Wilde set eyes on Lord Alfred Douglas. Indeed, the parallels were striking: a great genius, led into mortal peril by his passion for a handsome young fool with a glint in his trouble-hungry eye.

But this time there was no scandal. No

string of Piccadilly rent-boys recounting their days and nights of underage lust with 'Uncle Tony'. Because, simply, Tony Hart is beyond scandal. He's just too bloody nice.

He is also the greatest artist of his generation, a nose ahead of Francis Bacon and Rolf Harris. And just as Michelangelo and Raphael lit up the landscape of 16th-century Rome in their efforts to outdo each other, so it was Harris's bearded daubs that spurred Hart on to immortality.

Tony is currently working on the second series of *Smart Hart*. The legend lives on.
Richard Purvis

Mark & Lard

January 1997

"THOSE DREADFUL Northerners are terrible," said a blonde woman who works within spitting distance of the **loaded** office. "When is Chris Evans back?" Evans, from the popular commuter suburb of Warrington, was on holiday at the time and the mainstream breakfast Radio One audience were waking up to Radcliffe and Lard (aka Marc Riley), previously confined, after extensive market research, to the 10pm until midnight slot from Monday to Thursday. It came as something of a shock.

That is, to the loss adjusters and company representatives of the south east and not to Radcliffe and Lard. They made no concessions, continued to broadcast from the "Palace of Glittering Lights" (Oxford Road, Manchester) and won the love and admiration of anybody desperate to hear an accent and vocabulary other than the bland Radio One esperanto of Mark Goodier and Lisa l'Anson. To Northerners estranged in the south it was like the fall of Saigon. Welcome to Radio Freedom.

Whereas Evans has a studio posse of people culled from the cast of *Ever Decreasing Circles* (Jamie the student excluded), the new morning double act were all clipped Mancunian dialogue and agitated self-deprecating smart-arsey regularly interrupted by nationwide traffic information. One minute it would be "Alright our kid" and "Blimey Charlie", and the next it would be "In Suffolk, the A143 at Watersfield is blocked because of an accident and there is a diversion. Southbound on the M1 it's bad news from Luton to Harpenden."

It certainly is bad news from Luton to Harpenden. Straight after the weather (like the traffic information, broadcast in 'authoritative' home counties dialect) the

One minute it would be 'Alright our kid' and 'Blimey Charlie', and the next it would be, 'In Suffolk, the A143 at Watersfield is blocked.'

jingle, stolen from an interwar continuity announcer, cuts in, "This is the regional programme from the North and also the Empire programme." Radcliffe and Lard

were out of the blocks and taking the piss. Out of themselves mostly, although other DJs have their jingles bastardised and re-broadcast. They'd carry on in the same vein until 9am when "Funky Si" took over.

By that time, however, the punters had already heard both Wheel of Misfortune and Bird or Bloke? – where punters guess the sex of, for example Leslie Grantham and Leslie Judd – got dressed and left for work. They'd also listened to a half decent playlist and sketches which ranged between the frankly unamusing and the downright brilliant. Interestingly, the sketches are best when they fall flat on their arse because that provides the catalyst for the element which makes Radcliffe and Lard the best thing on radio and confirms their status as Greatest Living Englishmen.

Mancunians call it "having a pop". *Radio Times* features writers would, and probably do, call it "an incessant banter between the two, usually contradictory off-the-cuff nonsense but never less than inspired." At any given time a white noise argument can be transmitted into millions of homes like a bar room spat which has got out of hand. And then, all of a sudden, Radcliffe will cut in with "Shut up Lard for goodness sake." A slight pause and a faux-concerned, "Oh blimey Charlie."

It's hard to do it justice in print but it's all in the timing. For example, Radcliffe will begin a sentence, "*The Breakfast Show* biggie will be coming to you live at 19 minutes past..." Before, from the back of the studio, Lard will add, unnecessarily, "Eight." It is a master and servant type

arrangement but unlike Chris Evans and his acolytes, there's no clear focus. Lard is free, and in fact encouraged to interrupt and berate the man who is, in effect, his employer. He's a modern day Norman Wisdom.

The upstairs downstairs relationship is only present in the sense that Radcliffe has first option on the punchlines, unless

Unlike Cannon and Ball who favoured two straightmen, this is a double act without one and available for free on 97 to 99 FM.

'The Hapless Boy Lard' can go one better. Which, being hapless, he rarely does. A typical exchange:

Radcliffe: "Anyway, we won't be going as we are busy clubbing it."

Lard: "Clubbing a baby seal..."

Radcliffe: "No, we're going line dancing."

As a parody on the Chris Evans stunt of getting punters to turn up outside Broadcasting House, Radcliffe and Lard invite listeners to turn up outside the headquarters of BBC North on Oxford Road for the Wheel of Misfortune slot. Sometimes they get five people, mostly they don't.

The jingle starts, Lard looks out of the window:

Lard: "They're queuing already."

Radcliffe: "Are they?"

Lard: No. There are no contestants. There's nobody outside but there are two people outside Peppermill in Birmingham. And that's miles away."

Radcliffe: "Pebble Mill."

Lard: "Aye."

Radcliffe: "The Wheel of Misfortune will be coming up, contestants or not, in the last half hour of the programme. Has Bridy turned up in the canteen yet and Ernie from parcel despatch? That'll do nicely."

A trailer for Mark Goodier underlines the difference between the two shows and perhaps even the north and the south. It would be nice to think that, like Morecambe and Wise, Radcliffe and Lard go back to share a flat or a house where their radio roles are replicated and the "incessant banter" to-and-fros all day. Lard occasionally amusing Radcliffe and the latter attempting to maintain a professional distance, Radcliffe insisting that Lard fulfils his duties as fully paid up "sidekick and biscuit monitor"

As Lard notes in his self-penned biography: "To this day Radcliffe is regarded as one of the wittiest raconteurs on the wireless and Lard is regarded as a right royal pain in the arse by all those unlucky enough to be subjected to his relentless arsenal of half-baked catch phrases... Fancy a brew?... Cod, Fish Battered, Balls... Arse... Ho!... That's the bunny." Unlike Cannon and Ball who favoured two straightmen, this is a double act without one and available for free on 97 to 99 FM.

The north is ready to seize control of your radios. Then we want your televisions.
Bill Borrows

Patrick Moore

October 1997

MAGINE EXTRATERRESTRIALS having a close encounter with Patrick Moore. The aliens would surely conclude that the human race is the most eccentric in the galaxy and beyond help. Had Steven Spielberg cast Jeff Goldblum as a huge-arsed, monocled, baggy suited, squinting, xylophone-playing, brilliant-but-apparently-bonkers scientist in *The Lost World*, he'd have been ridiculed by the critics for introducing an outrageous and unbelievable caricature to the big screen.

Let's look at what Moore would call the "fects" about the world's maddest astronomer. First there's the monocle,

Moore sounds as though he's inhaled helium after taking several dozen amphetamines.

followed by that wild, squinting eye (the result of a motorcycle accident), those extraordinary bushy eyebrows, and a voice that rises towards the stratosphere as his peculiarly clipped, posh tones announce, "Good evening, and welcome to *The Sky At Night*." He is, after all, the fastest speaking man on television, gushing at a record 300 words per minute. He sounds as though he's inhaled helium after taking several dozen amphetamines.

Then there are his clothes. The 74-year-old Moore appears to have worn the same baggy suit and flapping tie for 40 years on *The Sky At Night*, usually with an upturned collar and sticking-up hair. He's a man who was born to have breakfast stains on his jumper. Only Patrick Moore could have accepted an award for the

worst-dressed man in Britain with the words, "Oh good show, there are some cranks about."

He's 6ft 3in tall, and even the baggiest suit can't disguise the fact that he has the biggest arse in TV history. Other TV personalities may talk a bunch of arse, but Moore appears to actually have a bunch of arses. As his late mother once said of him: "He was the untidiest, oddest little devil as a boy and he hasn't changed."

Predictably, Moore's political views are all stations to Barking, proceeding 30,000 miles west of Uranus. In 1979, he helped form the United Country Party. Its first candidate was one Lt Colonel Edmund Iremonger, a man who sounds like he shuffles round the house in army fatigues waiting for the balloon to go up.

Moore lives in a rambling thatched house in Sussex, and when he's not star-gazing, he's at the piano or composing works for xylophone. If you add details such as Moore's famous telescope sheds at the bottom of his garden, the cuckoo clock in his study, his housekeeper called Woody, the fact that he drives a 40-year-old Ford Prefect and rides a bicycle he bought when he was 10, then you have the complete picture of a man who could be a particularly deranged relative of Uncle Monty from *Withnail & I.*

The highlight of the

company for a few pints in his local pub, The Stargazer, named in his honour.

He's not adverse to a "gel", either. He was engaged, but his fiancée was killed a week before their wedding, by a bomb in the Second World War. He now maintains that, "Second best is no good for me." Had Moore married, he admits, "My life would have been totally different." A bit more earthly rumpy pumpy and he might never have devoted his life to his telescope sheds.

He perfectly embraces the spirit of the great English amateur. He has no poncey qualifications, being self taught in

As his late mother once said of him: 'He was the untidiest, oddest little devil as a boy and he hasn't changed.'

astronomy. Fax messages from NASA are often halted by his cat sitting on the machine. Patrick prefers antique telescopes to computer screens and says of the Internet: "My NASA chums keep telling me I should get on the Internet. I suppose I should learn how to use the thing... though, quite honestly, I can't be bothered."

Amid all the eccentricity, it's easy to forget that Moore has presented the longest running TV series in the world. In fact, he's never missed a show of *The Sky At Night* in 40 years, despite some bizarre accidents. When your mind's on the heavens it's not surprising that everyday life can become a little hazardous. He once slipped in the bath, hit his head and knocked himself out. Then there was the time a bluebottle flew into his mouth on live national TV. "I realised there was only one thing to do. I gave a strangled gulp, swallowed it, and carried on talking. Jolly unpleasant for me. But, as my mother remarked, even worse for the bluebottle."

Patrick Moore: the greatest living bluebottle-swallowing Englishman in the solar system.

Pete May

recent Mars landing was not Pathfinder's first pictures but Clive Anderson gently teasing Moore and re-running an old *Sky At Night* from 1957. Wielding what appeared to be several rotating dustbins tied together with bits of string, Moore and a bizarre, bow-tied chum called Claude desperately pointed their huge phallic telescope at the heavens. The moon, the planets and the stars were obscured by clouds. "This is really infuriating, there is nothing one can do" bluffed Moore, frantically padding for 20 minutes, suppressing a chuckle, and ending the show with, "From Brighton, where the sky is now completely overcast, goodnight."

Despite his vehement right-wing views, it's hard not to love a man who still uses words like 'bunkum' when dismissing astrology. Or who answered a letter from a Mr T Pott with a reply from A Jug, before discovering he'd wound up top scientist Thomas Pott. And a penchant for home brew and curry suggest he'd be good

Johnny Morris

July 1999

TO A LOT OF YOU, Johnny Morris was merely the man who gave giraffes and llamas a peculiar voice, a kind of twisted Dr Dolittle on a real life ventriloquist kick. And, although that alone would normally guarantee anyone a place on this page (despite the fact he was Welsh), his claim for a place is given even greater merit by the fact he never quit, went down sniping and, crucially, gave the world the musical delights of 'Juanita the Spanish Lobster', 'M4 – The Story Of A Motorway' and 'Cooey Louis' (a song about a homing pigeon).

Before *Animal Magic*, though, in which he played a kindly zoo-keeper who talked to the animals, Morris was a farm manager, a bailiff and, briefly (it was once assumed), a Nazi spy. He had, it seems, expressed a desire to be an English teacher in Hitler's Germany and was subsequently held under house arrest at the outbreak of World War II on the grounds that, among other things, he had been seen driving a German made Opel. I'm not making this up. Eventually, however, he was allowed to join the Home Guard, but even then fell under suspicion when he was overheard lending a red squirrel some kind of Germanic inflection.

After the war, the creator of the *Flowerpot Men* invited Morris to become the *Hot Chestnut Man*, a role he enjoyed

Both *Animal Hospital* and *Pet Rescue* were, Mr Morris claimed, 'enough to make you vomit'.

from 1953 – 61. During this period he also worked on a radio show entitled *Johnny's Jaunts* in which he talked to people as he travelled from Manchester to Torquay. It took him 20 weeks, and this, remember, was before Virgin Trains even started running the

West Coast line. But it's for his work on *Animal Magic* that he'll be best remembered, work that traded on the ability of its presenter to mimic certain exotic creatures. A measure of his genius is that, in the 22 years he fronted the show, not once did anyone complain that a llama would not sound like that,

People just assumed that whichever voice Johnny chose for the beast in question was almost certainly going to be perfect.

because nobody knew any better. People just assumed that whichever voice Johnny chose for the beast in question was almost certainly going to be perfect.

Had Morris, by chance, been suffering from laryngitis on the day he was due to provide a voice-over for the father figure to several shrimps in the Morecambe Bay area, the watching public would have taken it for granted that shrimps were fiercer than they'd previously imagined and, accordingly, the profits of Berni Inns would have gone through the floor. He was that important.

Or was he? To the vast majority he was just the mad old fella who talked to the animals, walked with the animals, walked, talked, and squawked with the animals. To his devoted following, it might come as something of a shock to realise that *Animal Magic* was actually shit, and that he only just makes the cut because of his anti-TV establishment, post-sacking rantings.

"*Pets Win Prizes* is disgusting," he once blathered. "Not pleasant for the animals and not nice to watch." *Animal Hospital* and *Pet Rescue* came in for much of the same. Both were, Mr Morris claimed, "enough to make you vomit". Clearly, he was not the kind of man to just lie down and die (until now, that is).

If something had animals in it and public sector broadcasting had any say in the project in the opinion of Johnny Morris, either he should have been presenting it, or both the decision-makers and the viewing public were clearly insane. It is this last-stage arrogance/self belief that shoe-horns him into the pantheon of berks and half-wits who constitute the Greatest Living Englishman hall of infamy. When the end finally came it was, despite his age (82), still quite unexpected. Johnny Morris: Welsh, not English. Dead not living. But indisputably one of the greatest.
Bill Borrows

John Noakes

July 1995

BACK IN THE SUMMER of 1973, a hellishly dull family holiday in Weston-Super-Mare was brightened considerably with my discovery that John Noakes of *Blue Peter* fame was due to open the local carnival. Along with a small army of fellow youngsters, I strolled along in eager anticipation of a glimpse of the pixie-faced daredevil whose understanding of tortoises was second to none.

Imagine then my delight when I found that Noakes was installed in his own tent and that the great man's autograph could be had for the price of a small donation to the Save The Badger Appeal. After queuing for an hour or so I found myself face to face with the man himself. However, no sooner had I opened my gob to express my long-standing admiration

than there was a shout from the back of the queue. "Oi, Noakesy!" some bright spark hollered, as he pointed in my direction. "That kid reckons you're a cunt!" Noakesy himself was unamused. "You're likely to grow up into a drug addict, an alcoholic and an all-round layabout." As it happens he was spot on in his predictions but I've never held it against him. Noakesy might have been conspicuous by his absence from television screens these past 15 years but my admiration for him has dimmed not a jot.

Every generation finds at least one action hero that it takes its hat off to and worships blindly. The younger shavers of today have their Schwarzeneggers and their Van Dammes. Back in the '70s John Noakes was indisputably the cat's pyjamas. As the resident have-a-go hero on *Blue Peter* it seemed that nothing was beyond him. One minute he'd be washing the arse of a baboon with expert sensitivity, the next he'd rustle up a 10-course banquet using a couple of toilet rolls and half a yard of sticky-back plastic. But it was his daredevil stunts that made him the toast of schoolyards up and down the land. He'd scamper up and down Nelson's Column, race down some treacherous stretch of river on an airbed, grapple with ferocious dingoes or throw caution to the winds and volunteer for a five-mile freefall parachute jump. His middle name was "Fearless" and we couldn't get enough of him. To impressionable youngsters of the time he was the zany uncle who would do anything for a laugh. And, unlike zany uncles in real life, he looked like a kind of bloke who could be trusted not to drag you into the long grass to tickle your goolies with a kestrel feather at a minute's notice.

What made Noakesy particularly endearing was the calm exterior he maintained in the midst of catastrophe. When, famously, an elephant called Lulu opened its arse-cheeks and sprayed the *Blue Peter* studio with half a ton of shit, Noakes waded through it with the carefree air of a man enjoying a leisurely Sunday morning stroll through the park. He was equally impressive when tumbling off a bobsleigh at 100mph attempting the famous Cresta Run at St Moritz. Asked by the BBC camera crew to show off the bruise on his parking space, Noakes calmly dropped his trousers to reveal a pair of sexy lace undies. "I'd borrowed them from my wife that morning," he explained with admirable cool. "Ran out of underpants, you see."

Particularly touching was the close relationship that Noakesy had with Shep, his black and white border collie. "Get down, Shep!" became his popular catchphrase. However, when Ed Barnes (BBC's head of children's programmes) insisted that Noakes could only have custody of his favourite dog if he wasn't used in television commercials, that calm exterior melted away to reveal an explosive temper. After threatening to knock Barnes' teeth down his throat, Noakes got to keep Shep and acquired another dog, Skip, for commercial work. "Shep was the best mate I ever had," a tearful Noakes announced when the dog finally croaked in 1987. "He was the one with all the talent. I was just his straight man. Believe me, that dog was a genius."

After 12 years with *Blue Peter*, Noakes finally departed in 1978. Then followed *Go With Noakes*, a hugely popular series which pursued Noakesy

> ## 'In real life I'm nothing like the happy-go-lucky buffoon on the telly. I'm sour and suspicious. I'm an awkward old sod. If that disappoints people, I couldn't give a damn.'

around Britain as he scaled new heights of derring-do. You were left with the impression that here was a man who would drink his own piss while dangling off the Severn Bridge if he was asked nicely enough.

Come the early '80s though and Noakesy announced his retirement from television. "I'm sick to death of the telly," he said. "It's a load of old rubbish." Ever the adventurer, he opted to sail around the Med in a 44ft sloop and had a merry old time of it until the boat broke up in a storm. Having been rescued by a Japanese tanker, he ploughed the insurance money into a bigger boat and sailed off to Majorca. Here he would settle and live the life of a virtual recluse until 1993, when he reluctantly emerged from obscurity to join the *Blue Peter* 35th anniversary celebration. However, when asked to reflect on his days as the one-man SAS team, Noakesy

refused to be overcome with dewy-eyed nostalgia. "It almost drove me potty," he seethed. "It was like living in a fantasy world. I had to invent this idiotic character to play and I resented that. The bloke on *Blue Peter* wasn't the real me. Noakes isn't even my real name. In real life I'm nothing like the happy-go-lucky buffoon on the telly. I'm sour and suspicious. I'm an awkward old sod. If that disappoints people, I couldn't give a damn."

Despite his reservations, the John Noakes revival was well underway. Last year, he was portrayed in an Edinburgh Festival play called *Gone With Noakes*. Membership of the Halifax-based John Noakes Appreciation Society tripled overnight. Now he is about to make a long overdue return to our screens, presenting a TV programme called *Third Avenue*, which will involve encouraging OAPs to take up adventurous sports.

"I don't see why the over 65s shouldn't have a go at white-water rapid riding and scuba-diving," he says. "Having said that, I don't take risks like I used to. Back in the old days I was like an overgrown schoolboy who enjoyed dicing with death just for a lark. As long as I felt I had a 60/40 chance of survival, I'd give it a go. But I'm past it now. The most dangerous thing I do these days is try my wife's recipes for Majorcan curry."

Jon Wilde

Richard Whiteley

September 1998

THE COLOSSUS OF WORDS. The king of Rich Tea smarm. The *Übergruppenführer* of the teribble pun. Richard Whiteley, head honcho on low-tech parlour game *Countdown*, is God in a bad tie. Yes, I know what you're thinking, this is the butane-addled ramblings of a daytime TV addict or some cunning Channel 4 propaganda designed to get you watching Whiteley's incompetent fumblings with increased awe. But no: Whiteley actually IS God. The master of creation, the lord of the apes, the big wobbly cheese. And all the evidence is there in front of you. Firstly, just like the big fella in the white beard, Richard actually created the universe. Well, the universe of Channel 4 anyway. Back in 1983, Richard's crippled grin was the first thing C4 viewers ever saw. "Let there be *Countdown*!" he said, and there was *Countdown*. "Let there be low-brow smut and racing from Doncaster," he added. And yea, the fourth channel was off,

The *Übergruppenführer* of the teribble pun, Richard Whiteley, head honcho on low-tech parlour game *Countdown*, is God in a bad tie.

falling over itself to deliver tits, smarm and the galloping gee-gees.

And ever since, just like God, Richard's sweaty mug has always been there, omnipresent, sliming across his chipboard 'n' Formica *Countdown* desk like a fat albino slug in a C&A blazer.

Alright, so there may be a few of you still out there – Christians for example – who are unable to accept Richard as your saviour, perhaps coming up with the pathetic argument that he is merely the most cack-handed presenter known to man, a geography teacher dressed up for the Christmas staff disco.

But as Sheena Easton so succinctly put it, nobody does it better. Richard Whiteley is as indispensable to life in the late 20th century as a wonky B&Q barbecue. Simultaneously indispensable and completely superfluous, Whiteley is *Countdown* personified: a poorly conceived mess that somehow just

works. Let's face it, without Richard Whiteley, *Countdown* would be *Turnabout*.

OK, so Richard's a fat sweaty lump with permafrost smile and a starter-motor laugh, but *Countdown*, nay, British culture would be a poorer place without him. He is part of a great British tradition of bumbling eccentrics: Will Hay, John Noakes, Magnus Pike, Prince Charles. He is as English as beans on toast simply because he knows he's poo and he's completely happy with it. Of course, I'm biased. I am among the select band of people lucky enough to have lived in the

Yorkshire TV area (read 'em and weep you mung-bean-guzzling southerners. YTV viewers get *Bullseye* and *Learn To Paint With Alwyne Crawshaw* piped into their stinking hovels daily). Yorkshire viewers don't just have to content themselves with *Countdown,* they also get to see Richard on the YTV evening news programme *Calendar,* talking about Guatemalan mining disasters and interrogating Michael Heseltine about the EMU. Imagine *that* shit.

In fact, it's a testament to Whiteley's unique place in the televisual world that he's actually managed to stay employed for over 30 years. The mystery isn't how he's such a big success – his cuddly idiocy was always going to be a big hit with the Parkinson's jitterbug crowd: a middle-aged man they could mother and conceivably fuck. Besides, plenty of people have made a career out of being shit at their jobs: just look at Frank Bruno, Louise Woodward or Princess Di.

But on *Countdown,* Richard Whiteley has grown beyond endearing incompetence like Dutch elm disease. For half an hour every day, the man is an utter wreck. Bad puns he can do. Mumbling and stuttering, fine. But faced with anything tricky like, ooh, starting the *Countdown* clock, Richard flaps about like

a cockatoo with one wing nailed to the desk. Beads of sweat break out on his forehead as he coughs, "OK... Let's, umm... let's start the rrrrr... round, erm 30 seconds from... um, now!" It's like he's suddenly mentally regressed to the age of four and he's forgotten all his lines in the school nativity play.

Perhaps his poor grasp of expression is down to having been taught English at

Simultaneously indispensable and completely superfluous, Whiteley is *Countdown* personified: a poorly conceived mess that somehow just works.

Giggleswick boarding school by that famous mangler of the language, Russell Harty. His sheltered upbringing might also go some way to explaining the ludicrous sexual tension between Richard and 'brainy temptress' Carol Vorderman. With an off-the-leather-cuff put-down or a mildly sultry look, Carol can reduce Richard to quivering blancmange, but

Richard always comes back for more, tongue flapping like a horny spaniel. It's a tea-time S&M party. Only last week a contestant came up with the six letter word 'goosed'. "Hmm... goosed..." mused Richard, visually straining his pasty shaped head for a joke. "Goosed, eh? Is that alright?"

"Depends who's on the receiving end, Richard..." quipped Carol.

In real life Richard is actually a bit of a smooth operator – and those of a nervous disposition may want to turn the page here – causing front page tabloid news last year with revelations of a 'steamy' affair with actress Kathryn Apanowicz, who once had it off with Dirty Den in *EastEnders.* Although, "It's not like he's some sort of stud, doing it five times a night," said one 'insider'.

But it is the crappy, stumbling Richard Whiteley, the porky polyester beanbag squirming like he's pissed in his seat who we love to watch as he reduces nine-year old *Countdown* champion Allan Saldhana to tears or turns bright purple as a contestant offers the word 'lesbian'.

Besides, if anyone needed any more proof that Richard Whiteley IS God, think about this: his name is an anagram of 'dirty wheelchair'. A big 15 points.
John Perry

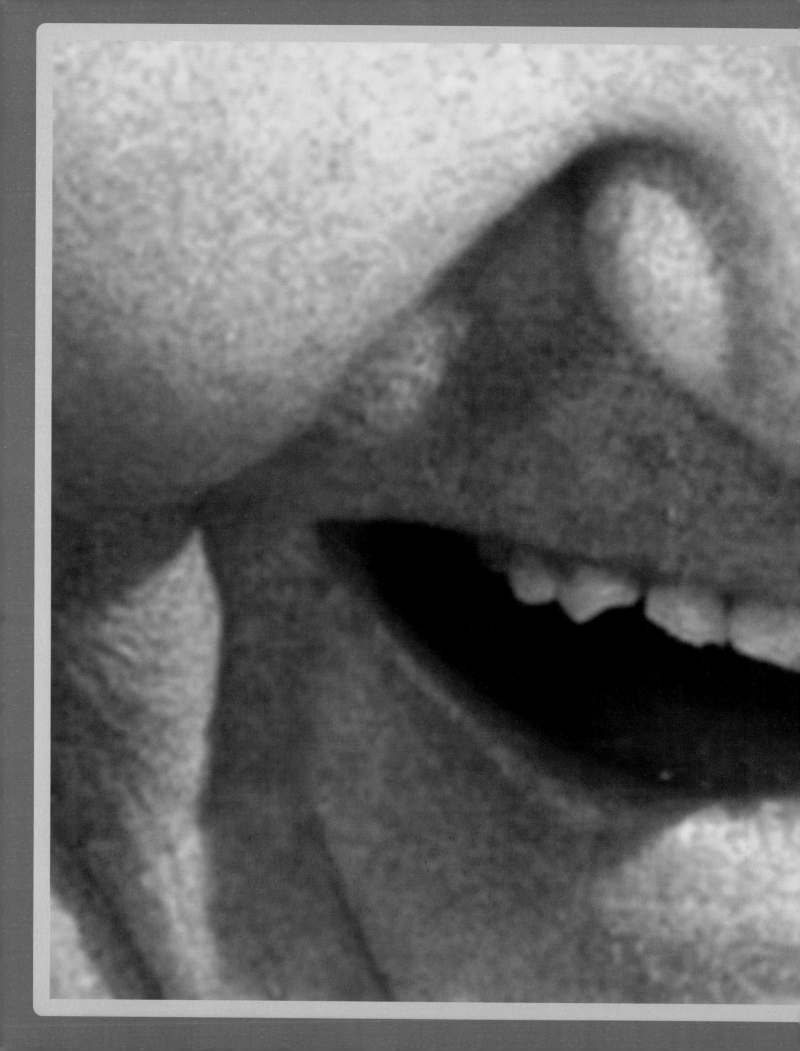

Luvvies

Patrick Allen

March 1995

YOU MIGHT NOT recognise Patrick Allen but you'll know his voice, it is *the* voice. The voice that's sold everything from cigarettes to cat food, the voice that would announce the end of the world, the voice of doom, the voice that's currently selling you Slimfast and Jungle compilations, the voice that announces: "And now, Britian's top light entertainer and newsagent, Vic Reeves." The voice of Patrick Allen.

Back in the '70s there was no more reassuring sight than Allen descending from the skies in a helicopter and being lowered into one of those timber-framed houses in the shade of an oak tree. You knew Barratt homes were worth having because Allen said so. His jaw and his voice were as good as a written guarantee. Something about him said authority, integrity, trust, and advertisers knew it.

Born in 1927 on a tobacco plantation in central Africa, Allen was the son of the Marchioness of Downshire. He went to school in Canada and, after a brief spell as a professional photographer of babies

You'll know his voice, it is *the* voice. The voice that's sold everything from cigarettes to cat food, the voice that would announce the end of the world.

in Hollywood, found his feet as an actor in Britain in the '50s. Allen's roles were as staunch as his bloodline. Hitchcock was the first to put him on the big screen, as a copper in *Dial M For Murder*, but his first big break was in the TV series *Crane*, playing the title role of a raffish but thoughtful Casablanca-based adventurer who did a bit of smuggling on the side.

As Vic Reeves recalls: "I first saw him in *Crane*, it was his swerving jaw that drew me to him... a very English jaw that moved like a banana. When we got on TV and had the choice of who did the voice it went without saying that it had to be Patrick Allen."

With the success of *Crane*, Allen was soon a national celebrity, most often described in the papers as 'Lantern jawed', 'craggy' and, on one occasion, 'moose-like'. His overall aura of rugged dependability led to his being known as 'TV's James Bond', a role he had in fact auditioned for but failed because "my jaw was too big".

The late '50s were boomtime for TV adverts and Allen swiftly rose to the top. By the late '60s he was known simply as 'The King'. Success had its rewards and Allen knew how to make the most of them. "I've had three Bentleys, two of 'em convertible and four different Aston

Martins in my time," he recalls. From the sauna of his mews house in Belgravia he presided over an electronics factory, business interests in the Middle East and his own voice-over studio in Soho. His appeal was described as: "A steely handshake, piercing blue eyes set in a craggy face, a dark brown voice and a hint of hidden violence." By 1976 he reckoned on having made over 3,000 voice-overs but felt that his career was "on the way down."

Having temporarily fallen from favour he toured the country giving lectures on the benefits of snuff taking. But the man was already an institution and he was soon back on the right track. 1978 saw Allen alongside Roger Moore, Richard Burton and Richard Harris in *The Wild Geese*, also appearing in Lewis Collins' finest hour, *Who Dares Wins*.

In 1980 Allen was picked to record the Ministry of Defence's announcement of nuclear war. "I can't say too much because of the Official Secrets Act. But I did it," says Allen. So how did it feel to be the voice of doom? "Fine, as long as I was around to hear it myself and pick up the residual payments, heh, heh, heh."

Four years later he had his first number one, repeating parts of the announcement on Frankie Goes To Hollywood's 'Two Tribes'. "Anything that's anti-war, I'm all for it. I think it took about six minutes."

And he's still going strong, the Barratt ads are back and Allen admits: "I'm having a bit of a renaissance at the moment, just back from Russia,

playing the M character in the new Michael Caine, Harry Palmer film." When he's not exercising his vocal talents you'll see him "on salmon rivers up and down the country".

Of his work with Reeves and Mortimer he says, "I think I'm a bit old and I don't understand what it's all about, but it seems very funny, maybe that's part of its charm. I'm sort of on their wavelength, I think it's a bit like Picasso in that it's impressionistic comedy."

In an uncertain world, there will always be Patrick Allen: dependable, professional, 40 years in showbiz and still delivering the goods. The last word goes to Vic Reeves. "He created that voice and everyone copied him. He's the leader of the pack. He's a brilliant bloke. No one could ever have a voice like that and a jaw to match. You can't beat him." Patrick Allen, we salute you.
Michael Holden

Robin Askwith

November 1998

MAGINE ROBIN ASKWITH on Tony Blair's New Deal scheme. He'd have rogered the bird at the Jobcentre in the interview room, while knocking over several trays of Restart forms. Arriving late on his first day in some workshop, he'd plead mitigating sexual congress with a female bus driver, get booted off the course for seducing a top female executive who looked like Joan Collins and then end up getting caught naked in the showers with a posh, unemployed sculptress also on a New Deal placement.

Luckily Timothy Lea, the lusty hero of the *Confessions* films played by Askwith, was putting it about in the era of full employment. Window cleaner, driving instructor, holiday camp entertainment officer, pop star: the world was his lobster. That's how Robin managed to shag endless women while wearing the dodgiest Y-fronts in cinema history.

In the 1970s and early '80s Askwith had the most famous arse in Britain. Everyone went to see the *Confessions* films, based on Christopher Wood's novels but rather like voting for Thatcher, no one would ever admit to it. *Confessions Of A Window Cleaner* started the chamois leather 'n' sauce fest in 1974, and three sequels followed: *Confessions Of A Driving Instructor*, *Confessions Of A Pop Performer* and *Confessions From A Holiday Camp*.

In Zimbabwe (then still Rhodesia), *Confessions Of A Window Cleaner* broke the box office record held by *Gone With The Wind* for the previous 30-odd years. With his open-mouthed startled 'ooh-er' expression, Askwith made the role of innocent young Timothy Lea his own, and he's still recognised in the streets for it to this day. But was he rewarded with several BAFTAs? No, he was so successful that in the poncey world of acting, the luvvies wouldn't touch him. His last film was *Britannia Hospital* in 1982.

When you see the films again (Channel 5's recently shown the *Confessions* films in the after-the-pub-on-Friday slot) what strikes you first is that they're far more *Carry On* in spirit than they are erotic. Sure there's nudity, but the sex is

It took a brave man to carry on being a window cleaner or driving instructor while all around were nymphomaniac housewives and posh birds dragging you into bed.

speeded up and dubbed with Benny Hill-style music or turned into a joke as Askwith's cheeky young pup is caught on the job submerged beneath foaming torrents from an overflowing washing machine. The *Confessions* films couldn't have been made anywhere but England. This was Britporn at its bashful best.

Askwith soon became a master of the single entendre. The style is summed up best in the scene where he's having tea with a randy mother and daughter and bites into a chocolate éclair – which spurts white gooey stuff all over the table.

It took a brave man to carry on being a window cleaner or driving instructor while all around were nymphomaniac housewives and posh birds dragging you into bed. *Confessions Of A Driving Instructor* has a classic scene where Robin's being seduced by an upper crust lady in a stately home when her husband

Robin managed to shag endless women while wearing the dodgiest Y-fronts in cinema history.

arrives back from hunting (with hounds) and tries to horsewhip him. A naked Timmy flees – covered only with a deck chair from a park – and arrives at the home of tasty older bird, Liz Frazer. She runs him a bath, strips to her black bra and panties and they fall fondling and frolicking into the bath. Only after a couple of slippery minutes a stray squeak reveals that Askwith has been shagging the rubber duck.

Some of our great character actors can be found in the *Confessions* films, which seem to include half the cast of *Till Death Us Do Part* and *It Ain' t Half Hot, Mum.* Even Tony Blair has a connection with Askwith. Anthony Booth, the 'Scouse Git' off Alf Garnett is Blair's father-in-law, and played Timothy's boss in *Confessions Of A Window Cleaner* and *Confessions From A Holiday Camp.* Dandy Nichols (Alf's 'Silly Moo') also appeared, as did the likes of John Le Mesurier, Bill Maynard, Irene Handl, Windsor Davies and George Layton from *Doctor In Charge.* Askwith even has a few gentle touches with a young Jill Gascoine in *Confessions Of A Pop Performer*, not to mention romps with Lynda Bellingham and later live-in girlfriend Linda Hayden.

While Timothy Lea was an unreconstructed oik, in real life Askwith went to Merchant Taylor's public school in Middlesex. Although he and a mate did once break into a shop and nick £200 worth of stamps – which they later returned – and one of his 'pranks' involved putting the headmaster's car on the chapel roof with a crane. (The stuff they teach you at toffs' schools, eh?)

But at times, his life has mirrored the films. He admits that when in bed with a married woman (now a famous actress) at the Queen's Hotel in Leeds, her husband

arrived and he had to climb out of the window and hide behind one of the letters on the hotel sign. He then climbed through another window, apologised to the couple also in bed ("'It's perfectly alright', they said,") and then hid in a broom cupboard ("When I turned up for filming everyone said I stank of furniture polish").

Askwith may have started out as a respected serious actor – his first film was Lindsay Anderson's 1968 classic *If...* but after 1982's *Britannia Hospital* there were only a few roles, such as the 1984 LWT comedy series *Bottle Boys* and a bit part in *EastEnders.* By Christmas 1997, Askwith was doing pantomine, starring in

Dick Whittington in Sheffield. He'd spent the last five years living unnoticed on the Maltese island of Gozo. His marriage to actress Leonie Mellinger had failed, and he was dating Mary, a beautician from Bournemouth. He told *The Mail on Sunday*: "I don't want to sound bitter but the producer Michael Rudman once said to me 'Robin, do you know what your trouble is? You played that role too well.'"

But he that is last will later be first. Sod the sniffy world of British film. The Askwith revival is here. *The Confessions* films are being re-released by Cinema Club this month, and like the *Carry On* films their credibility has been restored in the post-PC world. People might even realise that Robin can act a bit. Yes, Askwith's arse and even his underpants will surely soon be the subject of poncey post-modern seminars at London's ICA. Robin Askwith, we salute you. The greatest pair of buttocks ever seen on an Englishman.
Pete May

Tom Baker as Dr Who

May 1997

TOM BAKER was the longest serving and greatest *Doctor Who*. From 1974 to 1981, that wide-eyed grin was what Saturday tea time was all about. First came football results on the *Grandstand* teleprinter, then the news, *Basil Brush*, and finally the Doctor.

Everyone remembers the scarf, it was a multi-coloured woollen affair that was so long it was wrapped round his neck three times, no doubt the gift of some awful Gallifrey aunt. Baker's costume was perfect. The Doctor might have known all

> **Baker thwarted Davros simply by throwing his hat over a Dalek's eyepiece, causing it to go mental shouting 'Vision impaired!' before falling down a mineshaft.**

about time and relative dimensions in space, but his dress sense made Nigel off *EastEnders* seem suave. He merged care in the community chic with a mad Oxford don's cast-offs.

It was the perfect outfit to emphasise his childish enthusiasm and eccentric but brilliant persona. There was an ancient brown greatcoat with bags of jelly babies in its pockets, a brown cardigan, a lecturer's maroon cord jacket complete with elbow patches, tweed trousers and a battered old hat which certainly proved useful in 'Destiny of the Daleks': Baker thwarted Davros simply by throwing his hat over a Dalek's eyepiece, causing it to go mental shouting "Vision impaired!"

before falling down a mineshaft.

Baker did what any sensible Timelord would do when confronted by weekly armies of aliens bent on universal domination. He took the piss out of them. The appearance of some green wobbling monstrosity was always greeted with a smile and a cry of "Good evening!" or in the case of the Zygons, "Social call?"

"Awfully kind of you," he exclaims when a Movellian saves his life by zapping a Dalek about to exterminate him. When the brain of Morbious is brought back to life in a body made of butcher's bits with a giant claw and a goldfish bowl for a head the Doctor asks: "What's it like to be the biggest mongrel in the universe? Shouldn't you think of a new name? Pot pourri perhaps?"

And Cybermen could never appreciate a good joke. "You've got no home planet, no influence, nothing, you're just a bunch of tin soldiers skulking around the galaxy in an ancient spaceship," he told the Cyber leader in 'Revenge of the Cybermen'.

You'd think the Doctor would have been grateful that all these aliens had bothered to learn English. But no, when the Cyber leader says that he is going to "fragmentise" the planet Voga, Baker quips: "Fragmentise, I suppose we can't expect decent English from a machine."

The Zygons, lying under Loch Ness controlling a robot monster, also suffered. "Isn't the world a bit large for about six of you... You can't rule a world in hiding. You've got to come out on the balcony sometime and wave a tentacle."

Baker even used the classic viewers' joke about Daleks not being able to climb in one memorable scene. Having climbed a rope to another level he shouts at the pursuing Dalek: "If you're supposed to be the superior race of the universe, why don't you try climbing after us?"

Of course he had no idea how to operate the Tardis, being more a sort of Gallifreyan joyrider. The Doctor's sense of direction

made Mark Thatcher look like an ace navigator.

Then there were the companions. The Doctor was accompanied by tasty investigative journalist Sarah Jane Smith (Elisabeth Sladen) who was always fainting and being carried off by him, and, of course, Leela (Louise Jameson) who wore nothing but a skimpy animal skin throughout the galaxy.

Then there was posh blonde Romana (Lalla Ward) who never seemed worried

Everyone remembers the scarf, it was a multi-coloured woollen affair that was so long it was wrapped round his neck three times, no doubt the gift of some awful Gallifrey aunt.

when a weekend in Paris ended up as an encounter with Sacroth, the last of the Jagaroth. In fact she was so impressed with Tom Baker's sonic screwdriver that she married him. Sadly they later divorced and hot babe Ward married real life Doctor Who Richard Dawkins, who writes best-selling books about DNA but

probably can't name the dates of the Dalek/Movellan war.

Baker's Doctor was sometimes a little too much of a *Guardian* reader. In a classic scene from 'Genesis of the Daleks', the Doctor had the chance to destroy the Daleks at birth, but instead of exterminating the bunch of evil arse pepperpots came over like a *Late Show* critic: "Touch those two wires together and the Daleks are finished. Have I the right? You see some things might be better because of the Daleks, many future worlds will become allies just because of their fear of the Daleks... but if I wipe out a whole intelligent life form I become like them. I'm no better than the Daleks." And it would have buggered up the ratings too, mate.

Still, it takes a top Timelord to play with a yo-yo while he's got a Cyberman bomb strapped to his back, or indeed to disarm a Sontaran robot with a cry of, "Don't be afraid old thing, I'm not going to hurt you", before zapping it. And who else would have carried an umbrella on the planet Karn or told a Sontaran Grand Marshall planning to invade Earth, "Not today thank you!"

Tom Baker: you made the Doctor the greatest living Gallifreyan geezer in the universe. And you were the best ever advert for jelly babies too.
Pete May

Warren Clarke

August 1997

He embodies all the unrepentant nastiness of the vicious, thick as swill headbanger, possessed at best of a low cunning.

HIS FACE WAS ALWAYS far too good to be wasted on real thuggery. Stamped across a great, squat head are the eyes of a lizard, the snout of a truffle hog and the mouth of Jabba The Hutt. Real hooligans will often as not be rat-faced or angelic or simply nondescript, but Warren Clarke, with his mug like the anecdotal bulldog after a hearty wasps' nest breakfast, is the all-corners open champion of Albion screen brutality, the Great British Yob. He was born to smell of surly menace. If you saw Clarke coming towards you down a dark alley, your greatest fear wouldn't simply be getting your head put in. You'd experience the sudden horrific suspicion that you had warped into the strange yet semi-familiar world of the British movie, and that your bit-player expendability was about to translate itself into a grisly but unconvincingly stagey end. Despair of your equity card! It will not save you.

Unless you count a couple of lines in *The Virgin Soldiers*, which is exactly the sort of flick you'd expect him to turn up in, Warren Clarke's first movie role was as the aptly-named Dim, one of the bowler-hatted Droogs in the banned-in-Britain *A Clockwork Orange*. As pedigrees go, this is the screen bruiser equivalent of carrying in your veins the blood of half-a-dozen European royal families and a particularly well-bred line of dachsunds. Behind grotesque quantities of lipstick and enough mascara to daub *War and Peace* on the Great Wall of China, Clarke

'I have played some deeply, deeply disgusting people in my time,' Clarke once observed, with a certain amount of relish.

still looks like a psychopathic fuckpig with prehensile trotters capable of wielding a broken chair leg. He embodies all the unrepentant nastiness of the vicious, thick-as-swill headbanger, possessed at best of a low cunning that leaves him helpless beside the evil intelligence of Malcolm MacDowell's Alex. The chief Droog uses Dim as a part-time punchbag, only to have the snickering goon return as a policeman and wreak predictable bloody vengeance. Where Clarke goes, havoc will surely follow.

"I have played some deeply, deeply disgusting people in my time," Clarke once observed, with what seems like a certain amount of relish. Take *ID*, a more recent effort, in which Clarke appears as Bob, who might indeed be Dim 20 years on. Bob is a magnificent grotesque swathed with home-made tattoos, who rules the roost at The Rock, an East End pub somewhat less welcoming to non-regulars than The Slaughtered Lamb from *An American Werewolf In London*. This fearsome publican is also a middle-aged football hooligan of the type reputed to

suck out the eyeballs of their enemies, and speaks in a curious Yoda dialect otherwise heard only from Graham Taylor: "Tired am I of setting up rucks for plod to turn up only." The Force may not be with him, but he does keep an impressive baseball bat beneath the bar. Sadly we don't get to see him use it, as his much vaunted nose for bacon has failed to sniff out the undercover agent chatting up his barmaid: "Smell plod I don't," he announces satisfied. A shame, as it would be a great satisfaction to see him take the Louisville Slugger and see if he could make Reece Dinsdale's two-dimensional cop any flatter.

Clarke has impersonated Nazis, villains of one stripe or another, intransigent coppers, Quasimodo, Winston Churchill and, as he grows older, has cornered the market in bluff, rough-hewn businessmen, from an 18th century northern industrialist in *Blackadder The Third* to a 20th century northern industrialist in *Nice Work*. Given that Clarke was raised in Chorlton-cum-Hardy, voted town with the Most Stereotypically Northern Name in the 1993 All-UK Municipal Nomenclature Awards, it is hardly surprising that he has turned from ruck-happy yobboes to brash Lancashiremen as his stock-in-trade. He rescued the otherwise unwatchable 'tec serial *Dalziel & Pascoe* after one series featuring Hale & Pace in the hard bitten title roles – undoubtedly the worst case of miscasting since one-legged, 80-year-old French actress Sarah Bernhardt insisted that she was more than up to tackling Hamlet.

Don't be fooled by the gentle Bamber in *Moving Stories*, Clarke's real fortes are mono brain celled yobboes and pig-headed, gold-hearted, self-made men (see *The Manageress, Gone To The Dogs* etc). Clarke is so archetypally English he couldn't exist in life, and inevitably he doesn't. Not as we know him, anyway. Always well-mannered as a lad, he took artistic integrity to the point of (politely) telling *Coronation Street* to stuff their role. Twice. Dodging about to avoid being typecast, he gratifyingly failed. The real Warren Clarke is simply another actor, competent and principled. The Warren

Clarke of film and TV is either a mindless thug – *the* mindless thug – whose hideous spirit is conveniently chiselled onto his face, itself much like a bag of chisels; or an unprincipled wheeler-dealer whose swinish physiognomy conceals a gleaming sliver of conscience. He is no more real than village green cricket or drinkable English beer, but the idea of him is just as appealing. Warren Clarke is the dad Phil and Grant Mitchell seem never to have had. Truly, the ugly face of Britain. *David Bennun*

George Cole

September 1996

WHEN IT COMES to comic characters, you can't go too far wrong with the classic good-natured spiv; the lovable rogue with the twinkle in his mincers whose waking hours are spent ducking and diving his way around finer points of the law. Down the years, British comedy has thrown up its fair share of such endearing scoundrels: James Beck's Private Walker in *Dad's Army*; Ronnie Barker's Fletcher in *Porridge*; David Jason's Del Boy in *Only Fools and Horses*...

And then there's George Cole who, in a 50-year career, has made shady customers his celebrated stock in trade.

Having grown up on a South London council estate with his adoptive folks, the young Cole left school at 14 with nowt to look forward to except a job as a butcher's errand boy. Almost by accident

Decked out in camel hair coat and trilby, Daley might have been Flashy Harry's older brother.

though, he slipped into stage acting. Then, after being taken under the wing of the legendary Alastair Sim, he edged his way into films, making his debut in the 1941 spy caper *Cottage To Let*. However, it wasn't until 1954's *The Belles of St Trinians* that Cole made his first serious bid for immortality, playing the Fagin-like Flashy Harry opposite Sim's barmy headmistress. It was a role that fitted Cole like a glove and one which he successfully reprised in three other St Trinians films between 1958 and 1966. It would be a fair old while before Cole landed a role quite so side-splittingly memorable. In the meantime, he kept busy in radio, television and film – most memorably perhaps in the 1971 movie *Vampire Lovers*; a randy continental-style lesbian romp in which he was required in one scene to stroll around stark bollock naked while a couple of busty vampire dykes pleasured each other on a plush velvet carpet.

Then in 1979, Cole landed the role of Arfur Daley in *Minder*, one which would make him an instant folk hero up and down the land. Decked out in camel hair coat and trilby, Daley might have been

Flashy Harry's older brother – elevating the business of ducking and diving into something like an art form. Each week he could be found running some decidedly dodgy scheme from his Sarf London lock up, protected by his underpaid sidekick Terry (Dennis Waterman) who would be steered into some dicey predicament and end up completely wankered, while Arfur himself waited for the shit to hit the fan before making himself slightly more elusive than the Scarlet Pimpernel. Each episode invariably found the duo hooking up with a regular rogue's gallery of supporting characters including the mighty Brian Glover as the ne'er-do-well Yorky; George Layton as Des, the crooked garage mechanic; and Glynn Edwards as Dave, the unflappable gaffer at the Winchester watering hole where Arfur and Terry would retire to mull over the consequences of their latest scrape with the forces of law and order.

It was a predictable enough formula but one that rarely failed to strike oil by the tankerload. Between 1979 and 1985, when it was at its very best, *Minder* threw out more classic episodes than you could wave a shitty rag at in a full gale. There was 'Why Pay Tax?' (1981) when Arfur got on the wrong side of Johnny Taxman and was inspired to fake his own death and hole up in a seaside boarding house; and 'Poetic Justice Innit?' (1982), which offered a priceless parody of Sidney Lumet's

Twelve Angry Men with Arfur as the bent jury foreman. Perhaps best of all was 'Gunfight At The OK Laundrette' in which the long-suffering Terry is taken hostage by two militant rastas while Arfur does his best to exploit the situation for maximum financial gain – providing enough laughs along the way to gag a frozen maggot.

Waterman would later resurface in sitcoms that were so devoid of humour they should have been awarded a special blue plaque.

Around the mid-80s, the show started losing some of its gleam, appearing too ready to play it for laughs, while the plots started looking a bit too ungainly for their own good. By this time though, Arfur Daley was a certified national institution. And his nifty catchphrases ("'Er in... "a nice little earner", "A word i... like...") had taken up residence as part of the everyday lingo.

"It didn't really surprise me," said Cole, "that the character took off in the way that he did. Arfur was somebody that we could all identify with. He was a bit of a rogue, of course, but we could all

sympathise with him. And, of course, we all know someone a bit like him. I'm often asked whether he's anything like me. And I suppose he is. There's definitely a bit of Arfur Daley in me. And, if I hadn't got into acting, I'd have probably ended up a bit like him."

In 1991, Waterman decided he'd had a snootful of playing Terry McCann and opted to toss in the sponge – later to resurface in sitcoms that were so devoid of humour they should have been awarded a special blue plaque. For a while, *Minder* soldiered on with Gary Webster acting as Cole's weekly foil. Clearly though, the show was now edging past its sell-by date. And no one could have been too surprised when the plug was finally pulled in 1993 after more than a hundred episodes.

Through the '80s, though his name had become virtually synonymous with the Arfur Daley role, Cole still managed to prove that he was no one-trick pony. He was occasionally brilliant as Peter Bowles' devious estate agent brother in *The Bounder*. He excelled as the less than honourable MP, Sir Giles Lynchwood, in *Blott on the Landscape* – one episode of which found him tied naked to a chair, being whipped repeatedly by a rubber-clad hooker. More recently, he has starred as the Englishman, Henry Root in ITV's *Root Into Europe* and in *My Good Friend*, a superior sitcom in which he played an old geezer with a glad eye for the ladies. Then came his lucrative and hugely popular series of TV ads for the Leeds building society which have ensured that he'll be taking a crap on a solid gold chamber pot for years to come. And then there's his current ratings winner *Independent Man*, in which he stars as a scheming hairdresser with political ambitions.

Decent roles one and all. But, as sure as toast will land buttered side up, it's for Arfur Daley and his law-bending capers that George Cole will be remembered long after his toes have curled up. Sufficient reason then to get up off your fat chuff and raise a toast... Oi! Oi! Arfur! The world is your lobster, my son.
Jon Wilde

Lewis Collins

December 1997

Liverpool, rolling straight out of his mother's womb to bring a gun to bear on the midwife. Sixteen years later, following a spectacular dive through the schoolroom window, he took his first job, crimping at the Andre Bernard Salon, socking it to blue rinses and vanquishing unwanted perms. Early demos of 'She Loves You', played to him by Paul and his brother Mike McCartney, encouraged him to down his clippers and make the short step from hairdressing to rock 'n' roll. As a drummer and bassist in a flower power

Pulled over for drink driving, 'I gave the WPC the customary tour of the mobile home. We ended up spending part of Christmas together.'

cash-in band, the MOJOs, he spent the '60s noncing around dressed like a vaguely homosexual cowboy. Three top 10 hits later the band went belly up and Collins was forced to abandon the good life, and hand back his slinky Knightsbridge flat, flashy roller and topless models.

Acting seemed to be the next fastest route to fame, bags of cash and the requisite cheeky Suffolk villa. One of his first jobs was the role of playboy fop and syrupy bird charmer Gavin Rumsey in hit sitcom *The Cuckoo Waltz*.

"I was poofy in that," said Collins later, also maintaining that he could never see the humour in it.

By February 1977, he'd bought himself a trailer, which he was living in on theatrical tours: "I can eat there, drink there, and... well just about anything, if you know what I mean..." Before long he was pulled over for suspected drink

WHEN MY MUM first said she wanted me to be a professional I got the wrong end of the stick. I was diving around the front room of my Auntie's house in Basildon on Christmas Day, pretending to be Lewis Collins, Bodie to be precise. I had all the gear. Tooled up with more plastic weapons than Ann Summers, and giving it some to forces bent on the destruction of merry England's moral fabric. Namely the cat. I swear, even now, that if any Arabs had walked through my Auntie's front door with an idea of using her house as an HQ from which to rob the Bank of England, I'd have took 'em to pieces. And I wasn't the only nipper saving the world that morning. There were thousands of us who thought that *Who Dares Wins* star and Britain's premier action hero Lewis Collins was the best thing since *Bagpuss*.

Collins began life in Birkenhead,

driving. "I gave the WPC the customary tour of the mobile home. We ended up spending part of Christmas together."

Fame continued to lift its skirt in his direction, and later that year he auditioned to play the part of Mike Gambit in *The New Avengers*, losing out to coffee bean, knuckle-shuffler and housewives' favourite Gareth Hunt. Instead he took the part of ex-SAS man Bodie in a new action series *The Professionals*.

Britain's answer to *Starsky & Hutch*, *The Professionals* (first aired on ITV, 1978) were part of a spurious Government crime fighting unit called CI5. The motto of the unit was, "Meet violence with violence." With his ex-copper partner Doyle, played by Martin Shaw, the action lived up to the mantra. Plots were wild and furious. One week might involve German Terrorists holding Bodie and the vicar hostage, the next might feature a band of bank-robbing South African mercenaries. Action-wise it made every series that had gone before look and feel as exciting as QVC with the sound off.

Everyone from Joe Public to Princess Margaret thought *The Professionals* was top trumps and loved Collins because he literally took his work home with him. He'd pop up in the papers every week with his gun collection gobbing off about the 16 birds that he liked to have on the go at any one time. A crack shot with his own armoury of weapons and an expert in unarmed combat, he'd slipped into the Bodie role with ease – managing to convince large numbers of impressionable punters that he was the living embodiment of James Bond, John Holmes and Fritz the cat. A year after joining the series, he got sick of pretending and joined the Territorial Paras. By September 1980 he'd proved himself a mean enough bastard to win a coveted red beret from the regiment. Later, rumours abounded that he'd tried to join the Territorial SAS, but was apparently rejected on the grounds that he was a celebrity. You can't very well burst in a window just to have three terrorists turn round and say, "Fuck me, it's Lewis Collins!"

Later he was unsuccessfully proposed as a new Bond, though it was his role as Captain Skellern in the ropy SAS-ploitation movie *Who Dares Wins* that left his indelible boot print on British culture. Months were spent training with ex-SAS officers, yomping through the Brecon Beacons in preparation for the part. It was all a bit unnecessary.

"I'm ashamed to watch it, you can't take it seriously," he said later. "It's a joke... some officers of the SAS watched it and just laughed."

Everyone from Joe Public to Princess Margaret thought *The Professionals* was top trumps and loved Collins because he literally took his work home with him.

Now firmly typecast, he had lots of money, but nothing other than charity work to take up his time. With his massive fame starting to test his nerves, he was turning up on the front pages of the Sunday papers every other week, often claiming that he needed to be saved from all the birds. Once he arrived at a charity do with six minders, and was fined £300 for attempting to clear two workers from his own charity out of his house by firing a shotgun at his living room wall.

"Everything got on top of me," he said.

Soon his boozing and eating had grown out of control. A writer who lived with him while preparing a screenplay attested to his epic roast dinners, gargantuan fry-ups, and midnight double curries.

At a party at his country retreat in 1985, his girlfriend walked into the bedroom and found two barmaids snuggling up together. When she asked them if they wouldn't mind moving so she could get some sleep, Collins apparently came out of the bathroom and shouted, "How fucking dare you tell people what to do in my house! Get off my land!"

Soon, old conquests started to fall out of the trees like drunken monkeys. Ex-girlfriend Jessica Graham told the papers: "Lewis was great friends with the MP Norman St John Stevas and was often invited to his house when Princess Margaret was there. Once, when Lewis was the worse for drink, he kept saying to her, "Why do I have to call you Ma'am? Why can't I call you Margaret?" Everyone held their breath but the Princess just laughed."

In 1992, the 45-year-old hard-drinking womaniser married a 24-year-old blonde school teacher called Michelle Larret. 1985's Sexiest Man, the geezer with the motto, "A bird a day keeps the blues away", had packed it all in and tied the knot. It still isn't known if he entered the Church via the stained glass window and punched the vicar out, but it would have been cool if he did.

Phil Robinson

Britt Ekland

September 1995

N 1963 LITTLE BRITT EKLAND, a 19 year-old with the poise of an ice maiden and the lips of Venus, came to London on a modelling assignment. She was charmed, courted and, barely two weeks later, married to comedian come national institution Peter Sellers. Thus began a long running love hate affair between the Swedish siren and the simple, gagging for it British public. In the swinging '60s foreign birds, especially Scandinavian ones were a source of fascination and wonder. Everyone had heard the stories about the hot bed of unquenchable lust that lay behind their reproachful exteriors. Now there was a chance to find out if the tales were true. The *Daily Mirror* got very excited about the prospect. "She's like Bardot without the neuroses and awkward past," they panted.

In *Get Carter* she turned Michael Caine's tough man gangster exterior to putty by merely whispering some saucy stuff about her undies over the phone.

For a while Britt responded by playing it cool – a faithful wife and mother to Peter and little baby Victoria. The mayor of an Italian town did declare her a threat to public morality after the baring of what appeared to be her magnificent bum in a 1964 TV movie (it wasn't – up to her part as the ageing tart in *Scandal*, Britt always insisted on body doubles for shots below the belt). But Britt lost no time in hitting back.

"All this nonsense about Swedish sin," she said dismissively. "Swedish people

aren't like that. Now, Italian girls, they like to get married as quickly as possible and the same day go out and find an 'afternoon tea' lover."

The British public might never have discovered the full potential and dark mystery of the place they call Ek-land if the 19-year-old girl hadn't blossomed into a headstrong young lady. Fleeing her suffocating marriage with Sellers she was soon out and about, reliving her youth as a prototypical hippy chick of the permissive age. Britt was young, free and single, strutting down the Kings Road in bared midriff and mini-skirt declaring that she was off to make a movie with John Cassavetes "full of youth, protest and vigour".

Shortly after, confirming suspicions about what went on with Swedish girls when the lights went down, she revealed the heart attack Sellers had suffered during their marriage happened during a champagne and poppers sniffing sex session. The groundwork had been laid for the acme of Britt's all too easily dismissed acting career. In two of the great British classics of the '70s – *Get Carter* and *The Wicker Man* – she played integral, if wonderfully gratuitous, roles toying with and fulfilling all the foreign bird fantasies lurking in the British mindset.

In *Get Carter* she turned Michael Caine's tough man gangster exterior to putty by merely whispering some saucy stuff about her undies over the telephone line. In *The Wicker Man* she was unleashed, the toast of Scottish pagan outpost Summerisle, the landlord's daughter, mistress of sexual initiation and cheerleader holding a giant phallic symbol aloft for the local fertility rite. Edward Woodward's uptight lay preacher is reduced to a physical wreck by her naked, masturbatory, all night long dance in the adjoining room.

There were other roles around the same time – the comedy wench in *Flash*, clad in little more than a micro bikini as Roger Moore's sexy secret sidekick in *The Man With The Golden Gun,* and allowing 12 year-old Mark Lester to see and feel the full extent of her Swedish charms in

These days she's a (pretty appalling) novelist, Swedish chat show host and one of those people famous for simply being famous.

Night Hair Child – that made her new position clear. Laughably Britt was at the same time trying to get a campaign going for more family films. She said she only made the movies she did because as a single mum she had to do whatever it took to pay the bills. So like a true heroine she laid back, closed her eyes and thought of England, or perhaps Sweden. Whatever – we admired her courage in the face of adversity.

Since then the affair between Britt and the Brits has run hot and cold. She's had to defend herself against allegations that motherly neglect helped cause little Victoria's descent into the sordid LA world of a Heidi Fleiss-run prostitution ring and coke dealing. She's been bulimic and anorexic, succumbed to the surgeon's scalpel and she's suffered the wrath of sad Rod Stewart fans who reckon that during their time together big bad Britt turned the poor wee Tartan laddie's head. How easily they forget that it was Britt's image management that helped Rod become an American superstar. Who understood better than she that the way to the public's heart was through a man's leopardskin tight trousers?

Anyway, Britt, who has romanced and married the rich (record mogul Lou Adler), the mega famous (Warren Beatty, "a very quick lover" she pointedly told the press), royalty (Lord Lichfield), numerous toyboys and rock 'n' roll has-beens (Big Jim Stray Cats and Rod Stewart), couldn't care less. She's kept her head above water and fulfilled all her 19-year-old dreams. These days she's a (pretty appalling) novelist, Swedish chat show host and one of those people famous for simply being famous. And, having passed her half century, she doesn't even have to play it cool anymore. "Today, every man carries a condom. It really is a joy to be single," she recently told reporters.

Spoken, as they say, like a true Brit(t).
Gavin Martin

John Hurt

September 1997

"CAN'T YOU SEE I'm fucking drinking? Now fuck off and leave me alone!" Finding myself in London's West End back in the summer of 1988 with an hour to kill, I'd wandered aimlessly into some low down Soho watering hole, where I found myself gazing down in some awe at the hugely dishevelled figure of John Hurt. Slumped on a bench with a smouldering Gitane in one hand a large tumbler of rotgut in t'other, you would not have needed to consult your *How To Tell If A Man Is Drunk* manual to ascertain that this particular man was, indeed, as drunk as a skunk in a trunk. And, what's more, not in the mood for any messing. Then, spotting the inky biro in my hand, he suddenly changed his tune. "Oh, you're

'The best thing about success,' Hurt said back in the early '70s, 'is that it enables you to afford a better class of alcohol.'

just an autograph hunter! How fucking delightful! I thought you were one of those hyenas from the press. Now, if it's just an autograph you're after, kindly refill my glass, pull up a chair and I'll tell you some jokes funny enough to blow a buzzard off a shit wagon." Which is

precisely what he continued to do for the next hour and a half, a bravura performance all in all. Not that that should come as any great surprise. 'Cos, in more ways than you could scare the crows off a cabbage patch, John Hurt's

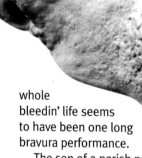

whole bleedin' life seems to have been one long bravura performance.

The son of a parish priest, the young Hurt endured a harsh, grim upbringing in Anglo-Catholic schools, which firmed up his resolve to have no truck whatsoever with convention. He discovered a liking for the acting game while still at school and, after passing through the ranks of RADA, was off to a flyer with the role of the wrongly executed Timothy Evans in the classic *10 Rillington Place*, the first of many rattling performances that he would notch up over the years. *A Man For All Seasons, The Elephant Man, Midnight Express, The*

Hit, 1984, Alien, Scandal, The Field, TV's *I, Claudius, The Naked Civil Servant*... if we were to name all of Hurt's gilt-edged moments, we'd be here all sodding night.

Of course, he's checked into his fair share of turkey farms – most notably *Heaven's Gate*, which remains one of the biggest box office calamities of all time. But when he's good, he's nowt short of dynamite. And, like all the world's top actors, Hurt's greatness on the screen appears almost entirely effortless. His gloriously flamboyant outing as Quentin Crisp in *The Naked Civil Servant* made him famous overnight. Around this time, in the mid-70s, he was being spoken of as the natural heir to the likes of Dickie Burton and Alec Guinness. However, top-drawer Hollywood success always seemed to just elude him. One got the impression that Hurt never gave a monkey's nuts either way. "I love to be involved in good work," he once said. "But I'm not that ambitious. I'll work hard, but it's just as important to me to have a fucking good time while I'm doing it."

Over the years, he became just as renowned for having "a fucking good time" as he was for his acting abilities. He always did like a drink, did Hurt. "The best thing about success," he said back in the early '70s, "is that it enables you to afford a better class of alcohol." His regular week-long benders would be followed by periods of strict abstinence and solemn promises that he intended to give up the sauce for good. "Not today," he was fond of saying. "But definitely tomorrow. No more drinkies for me. From now on, I'm going to be a good little boy." And, in less time than it takes to say "Same again barman," he'd be ripped to

the tits all over again. "I just love to drink," he once said. "Life is just so fucking boring, I simply refuse to drink in moderation. If that means that I sometimes behave badly, then so be it."

Down the years, he's managed to turn behaving badly into something like an art form. Like the time he reportedly got completely shit-faced at a top nobs' polo match and unashamedly started chatting up a wholly bemused Princess Di. Then came his jugged-up performance at a top London hotel following 1989's prestigious BAFTA awards when, finding himself completely and utterly parboiled, the old roisterer wandered around the hotel singing hymns and attempting to plant kisses on the assembled guests – male and female alike. He progressed to playfully wrestling with passers-by. Then it all turned a bit unsavoury. Clearly in the

Top-drawer Hollywood success always seemed to just elude him: one got the impression that Hurt never gave a monkey's nuts either way.

mood for a bit of a scruff-up, he raised his fists and yodelled, "Come and get it you fuckers! Which bastard wants it first? C'mon, you fucking cowards, let's see what you're made of." By way of an encore, he ended up spread-eagled on the floor after tumbling down a flight of stairs proclaiming, "I'm a bad boy and I fucking love it."

One of the true roaring boys – no two ways about it – and a *Greatest Living Englishman* by any reckoning. Great? Decidedly. Living? To the flaming max. Englishman? Well, more or less. As Hurt himself puts it, "I'm a half-Irish, half-Scottish, English actor." And a top one at that. John Hurt is welcome to piss on our boots and tell us it's raining. Any old time.
Jon Wilde

Christopher Lee

November 1999

CHRISTOPHER LEE must wake up every morning and curse his bad luck. There he was, all set for world domination for the 20th time and up pops Roger Moore and puts a bullet in his third tit. He'd already failed in his attempt to dress up like a Chinaman and take over the world with a bunch of drug-crazed saucepots, with poisoned lips. Not only that, but every time he got a good thing going with a bunch of big-toothed Goth women and heaving-bosomed virgins, someone always spoiled it with a nasty sharp stick. Buggered if he wouldn't have gotten away with it, too, if it hadn't been for those meddling kids...

When you think about it, Englishmen play rather good villains. In recent years Hollywood has paid good money to ship some of our finest actors (Rickman, Oldman, Roth) over to Tinseltown to ham it up as the bad guy in top-dollar action films. Perhaps it's something to do with the Yanks' perception of Englishmen as cold and unemotional posh blokes. But

'It is my responsibility to persuade people to turn away from black magic.'

no man, English or otherwise, has played the villain quite so well as posh, cold, unemotional Christopher Lee. He's played it so well, in fact, that it's pretty much all he's done his whole career.

We're not just talking villains, either, we're talking Super Villains. Dracula, for starters. Frankenstein's creature, the Mummy, The Man With The Golden Gun, evil high priests and excommunicated padres, Fu Manchu, Rasputin, The Mad Monk and Prince Philip – Christopher Lee's played them all with the kind of brutal, hard-staring tyranny you normally associate with festival security.

Born in Belgravia, London in 1922, Christopher Frank Carandini Lee was the son of an Italian Countess who could trace her lineage back to the first century AD. His childhood, as Mike Myer's Dr Evil might say, was typical: summers in Rangoon, society garden parties etc, until his stepfather blew all the family's money. Young Chris worked in the City for a bit before serving in the RAF and Special Forces where he was decorated for distinguished service. After the war, and set upon an acting career, he initially found it difficult to break into decent roles as, at 6ft 4in, he was considered too tall and 'foreign looking'. His real break came in 1957 in *The Curse Of Frankenstein*, the start of a long and fruitful

association with Hammer studios. A year later he would first play the role for which he is still most famous, Dracula.

In total he played the character eight times, but despite being the most memorable and charismatic Count going, he was never comfortable with the typecasting it brought him, as it had done '30s Dracula Bela Lugosi. At one point, Lee couldn't go anywhere without people behaving as though he was about to consign them to eternal night. On holiday in Bavaria, the proprietor of a restaurant brought him a bowl of blood: "I sat there, looking at the bowl and at the proprietor who was obviously very worried," he recorded. "So I drank it."

But if the general public couldn't separate his characters from his real persona, he seemed to lose the plot a bit himself on occasion. Following characteristically spooky roles in top Dennis Wheatley black magic films *The Devil Rides Out* and *To The Devil A Daughter*, Lee claimed in a national newspaper in 1978 that Middle East conflicts were caused by black magic: "I feel it is my responsibility to persuade people to turn away from black magic. I think my films do just that by showing audiences the true horrors of evil," he blathered.

It wasn't all supernature for Lee, though. In 1965 he starred in the first of the Fu Manchu series of films, in which he played a mad mandarin with a crazy moustache and a car boot load of ludicrous plans for world domination. But the comedy didn't stop there. In an attempt to prove he could be funny as well as scary, he later hosted *Saturday Night Live* with Dan Ackroyd and John Belushi, which led to unfortunate roles in

Spielberg's *1941*, *Police Academy 7* and as Phil the Greek in *Charles & Diana: A Royal Love Story*.

In 1974 he was called upon to become Bond villain Francisco Scaramanga in *The Man With The Golden Gun*. Lee was actually a step cousin of Bond creator Ian Fleming, who conceded that Scaramanga was one of his weakest villains. Lee took the role and made it his own, transforming Scaramanga into what he described as a "counter Bond", a suave, well dressed and unflappable anti-hero rather than the more thuggish character Fleming had written. Lee played the super villain as super-cool despite having three nipples and a dwarf sidekick with a creepy Oompah Loompah vibe.

At one point, Lee couldn't go anywhere without people behaving as though he was about to consign them to eternal night.

But it is his 1973 role as Lord Summerisle, the mad-haired, kilt-wearing pagan Scottish laird in *The Wicker Man*, which he considers his best. Unflappably twisted in the face of Edward Woodward's uptight Christian copper, Lee pulls off a film-stealingly sinister performance while naked young girls cavort outside his window. Fantastic.

It is, coincidentally, the only film in which his bad guy triumphs. With the sweet smell of success and barbecued pork in his nostrils, he stands at the end of the film, arms aloft, crazy hair flapping triumphant at last. It was a fleeting success, but really you can't knock a man for trying. It's just this kind of British perseverance and unflinching megalomania that built our Empire and got us 13 years of Thatcherism. Christopher Lee, Greatest Undead Englishman, and you can't argue with that.
Chris Burke

James Mason

April 1998

HE WAS FAMOUS for a fair number of things, was James Mason. For starters, he was the only famous person ever to come out of Huddersfield. He was also a top-notch actor who appeared in gobs of great films, including *The Odd Man Out, A Star Is Born, North By Northwest, Desert Fox,* *Lolita* and *The Verdict*. That's all common knowledge, is that.

What is less well known is that James Mason had a ferociously hairy back. The hairiest back in Hollywood, so it is said. Even hairier than Bogart's or Chaplin's, which is saying something. "As hairy as a bear trapper's hat," according to one of the many sex kittens Mason got to know in the biblical sense during his time in Hollywood. So incredibly hairy was Mason's back that he was asked to show it off at all the top Hollywood parties. Being a shy man, he would politely decline.

It is unclear whether Mason was actually born with a hairy back. Or whether his back started getting hairy later in life. What is sure is that it was in an advanced state of tuftiness by the time he made his theatre debut in 1931. We

'There were times when he wore the look of a man who had just strangled his mother-in-law and was attempting to look as though he'd spent the morning picking blackberries.'

know this because a stage manager called McNulty was heard to remark: "That man Mason is no slouch when it comes to acting, but Great Scott! What a hairy back he's got!"

Mason made his film debut in 1935's *Late Extra*. But the hoi polloi would have to wait another eight years before they were treated to a glimpse of his legendary furry back. This occurred in 1933's *The Man In Grey*, when, shortly after the scene in which he horsewhips Margaret Lockwood, Mason removes his shirt, to reveal a back that is monstrously, child-frighteningly shaggy.

By this time Mason had become famous for playing gentlemanly villains. Snobbery with menace, that was his stock-in-trade. Nowhere was this menace better demonstrated that in 1946's *The Seventh Veil*, when he smashed co-star Ann Todd's fingers with a hammer – a scene which prompted the Soviet Minister for Higher Education to declaim, "Mason is celebrated for the refined cruelty with which he tortures women on the screen. He is an instance of decadent and poisonous Western culture."

That's as may be. Whatever, it didn't stop him becoming the top male box office star of the era. At least in England. In America they didn't know him from a pig in a poke. So it was off across the big pond that he hopped, meaning to launch himself as a bona fide matinee idol. "I desperately wanted to be an overnight sensation," he would later say. But it didn't quite work out like that. "For the first five years, I felt like a man who was shooting arrows into the air and missing every time." B-movie flop followed B-movie flop. Then, in 1951, he starred in Albert Lewin's *Pandora & The Flying Dutchman*. From then he watched his career take off like a blowtorched stoat. For the best part of 10 years he couldn't put a foot wrong. He was sly-eyed Captain Nemo in *20,000 Leagues Under The Sea*, a double-crossing Brutus in *Julius Caesar*, a shifty villain in Hitchcock's *North By Northwest* and a dissolute junkie in Nicholas Ray's *Bigger Than Life*. Not to mention numerous flicks in which he strutted his stuff as a mad Nazi – a particular favourite being the notorious Afrika Korps general and bottom-pincher Erwin Rommel.

A good run by anyone's standards, during which time Mason honed his brooding style to near perfection. He could brood with the best of 'em, could Mason. "There was something electric and at the same time very dangerous about him," said Ann Todd. His biographer Sheridan Morley highlighted his "dark and mystic sexuality". Director Michael Powell was to recall him as a "dark young god" with "a voice and bearing second to none". Said director Sidney Lumet, "There were times when

he wore the look of a man who had just strangled his mother-in-law and was attempting to look as though he'd spent the morning picking blackberries."

Off screen, he fashioned himself as a fully paid-up member of the Gentlemen Breed. Blazer, grey flannels, everything just so. Good manners were a speciality. Mason was so polite he wouldn't open an

oyster without knocking on the shell first. That said, slagging off other members of his profession was something of a hobby. He once described Raquel Welch as "the kind of woman who wouldn't know chicken shit from chicken salad". Of Barbara Rush, his co-star in *Bigger Than Life*, he said: "Cinema needs her like Beethoven's Fifth needs a one-armed banjo player."

Through the '60s and '70s he delivered his fair share of stinkers, but there were enough classic performances along the way to keep his reputation in the pink. He was a perfectly slimy Humbert Humbert in Stanley Kubrick's *Lolita*, and an oily Nazi in *The Blue Max*, *Cross of Iron* and *The Boys From Brazil*. By the '80s he had established himself as one of the finest

character actors in the business. He was outstanding as the unscrupulous lawyer menacing Paul Newman in 1982's *The Verdict*, and superb as the crotchety landowner in *The Shooting Party*.

It was in the latter that audiences were treated to a rare glimpse of his naked back – which, by this time had become so hairy that he might easily have been mistaken for a man giving a piggy-back to an unusually hirsute gibbon. It's said his wife had to trim it daily with garden shears.

In his later years Mason lived in Switzerland, and by all accounts he became a bit of a strange old cove. Increasingly absent-minded, he was known to climb into the bath without removing his clothes. He also became addicted to cakes.

Friends observed that, late in life, he seemed obsessed with the idea that he'd never fulfilled himself as an actor. As Sheridan Morley remarked, "He remained a deeply troubled, enigmatic and often unhappy man, living in a curious kind of internal exile from which he would occasionally emerge to wish that he were somewhere else."

He had it all: a voice like fresh cream poured over hot gravel, and a back as hairy as they come.

Maybe he never became a solid gold superstar. But Mason put in enough first-rank turns over the years to be considered one of the great screen actors of the century. He had it all: a voice like fresh cream poured over hot gravel, and a back as hairy as they come. He's dead now, of course. But his legend lives on. And it would be nice to imagine that, as we speak, he's up there in that happy hunting ground reserved for first chop-actors, the fungus on his back growing thicker and longer by the minute.

Jon Wilde

Bill Maynard

October 1994

TRULY ONE OF THE CHAPS, Bill Maynard always knew which side his bread was buttered. "At the height of my fame," he says "I had the lot. Plenty of cash, flashy cars, an astonishing-looking bird on my arm at all times. The fact that I was married didn't stop me living my life to the hilt. I was a boozer, a gambler, a hopeless philanderer, an all-round reprobate, everything a husband shouldn't be. I was always loud, large, happy-go-lucky and bugger the consequences."

Though best known to the younger generation as the scruffy geezer from TV's *Heartbeat*, Maynard's showbiz career now spans 40 years and has offered him more than a few choice highlights. Starting out as a child circus performer, it wasn't long before he was taking advantage of his chubby good looks that made him irresistible to women: "I lost my virginity at the age of 11. All that I can really remember about it was that it occurred somewhere between Leicester and Sheffield in the back of a Ford Popular. She was a circus contortionist which was pretty handy in the circumstances."

In the '50s, he graduated from singing in clubs to acting in top West End shows and generally took his pleasure where he could find it. In his 1975 autobiography, *The Yo Yo Man*, he describes the advantage of sharing a flat with five gorgeous showgirls: "On one memorable occasion, we all returned to the flat, rather merry after a night on the town, I retired to bed and heard the sound of giggling coming from the next room. Suddenly my bedroom opened and five beauties stepped in... stark naked. One of them said: "OK Bill, lets see what you're made of," and they all jumped into my bed. Imagine five beautiful women writhing all over you. I could have died of

happiness. It would have taken a week to get the smile off of my face and a full month to get the lid on the coffin."

Maynard rose to television fame playing the straight man to Terry Scott in *Great Scott – It's Maynard*. Through the late '50s and '60s his career took in radio, variety, theatre and cabaret. But it was his film and TV work in the '70s in which established Maynard as one of the leading blokes of the age. After playing Alf Garnet's next door neighbour in the film version of *Till Death Us Do Part*, he starred in six *Carry On*s (most notably as Guy Fawkes in *Carry On Henry*), three *Confession* films, as well as appearing in film versions of both *Bless This House* and *Man About The House*. In the same

period, he also enjoyed a brush with pop celebrity, his recording of 'I'm Not A Pheasant Plucker, I'm a Pheasant Plucker's Son', reached the dizzy heights of 168 in the charts despite being banned by the BBC.

His '70s TV career took off with a plum part in Dennis Potter's *Paper Roses* and continued with the role of roguish pub singer Mickie Malone in *Coronation Street* and an award-winning performance in Colin Welland's *Kisses At Fifty* in which he played a married bloke who runs off with a busty barmaid. Then came *The Life Of Riley*, the first in the trio of classic sitcoms, in which he played a hapless insurance agent coping with a troublesome son. This was followed in

1975 by Roy Clarke's *Oh No! It's Selwyn Froggitt,* arguably the height of Maynard's brilliant career. Here, over the course of 28 episodes, he excelled as the accident-prone handyman who saw himself as something of an intellectual despite that his idea of culture stretched no further than the local bingo hall. Every episode seemed to involve a great deal of falling off ladders and down man-holes and tripping over shoe-laces. At every opportunity, Maynard would raise his thumb aloft, grin foolishly and utter his popular catch-phrase, "Magic!"

The formula proved highly popular and confirmed that, even in his fifties, bald as a billiard ball, and weighing close to 19 stone, Maynard still had whatever it took to moisten ladies' gussets up and down the land. At the height of the show's popularity, he claimed to have received piles of letters from virginal young women offering him large sums of cash if he would deflower them, along with irate

'I was a boozer, a gambler, a hopeless philanderer, an all-round reprobate, everything a husband shouldn't be.'

notes from husbands who caught their spouses masturbating with broken chair legs and Guinness bottles whilst watching *Selwyn Froggitt.*

After playing the bungling boss of an engineering firm in *The Gaffer,* Maynard slowly faded from the TV screen, devoting his energies mainly to theatre and pantomime. Now in his sixties and married for a second time (to widow of speed ace Donald Campbell), he appears to have put his crumpet-chasing far behind him. "When I was a young lad," he says, "I had tremendous drive for chasing birds. But they take some catching and I'm no spring chicken. I'm glad to have given all that up but that's why I'm probably so fat these days. I just don't get the exercise like I used to."
Jon Wilde

Patrick McGoohan as No 6

July 1997

"WHERE AM I?"
"In the village."
"What do you want?"
"Information."
"Whose side are you on?"

"That would be telling. We want information."

"You won't get it."

"By hook or by crook we will!"

"Who are you?"

"The new Number Two."

"Who is Number One?"

"You are Number Six."

"I am not a number, I am a free man!"

Even Jeremy Paxman would have struggled to get information out of Number Six. Patrick McGoohan was a stroppy bugger in *The Prisoner*, but he did give us the most memorable opening sequence in TV history.

Cults are made of such things; The Village's numbered penny farthing badges, Patrick McGoohan's piped blazer, The Village Mini-Moke taxis, Number Two's college scarf, the giant white bubble

'You are Number Six.' 'I am not a number, I am a free man!'

called 'Rover' chasing inmates on the beach, the Village greeting of "Be seeing you", the bizarre setting of Portneirion in Wales, and that classic '60s theme music.

Poor old Number Six. One minute he's banging his fist on the table telling his employers that life in the secret service is a bunch of arse. He's looking forward to signing on, a few lie-ins and some totty that isn't a KGB honey trap. The next moment a dwarf gases his pad and he wakes up in somewhere called The

Village and everyone wants to know why he resigned.

Patrick McGoohan as Number Six was a hero to anyone who has ever refused to conform. Even while being pumped full of drugs, lobotomised and chased along Welsh beaches by a giant white bubble,

McGoohan still heroically maintained that he was a free man.

There he was, trapped in the ultimate suburbia. Imagine the world run by *Woman And Home* and you have The Village. Everyone was superficially happy; but beneath the brass bands, arts and crafts societies and brightly coloured umbrellas, anyone who deviated from the norm was found guilty of disharmony by the committee, sedated and given a quick lobotomy known as "instant social conversion".

In a seminal episode Number Six was declared 'unmutual' as part of The Village's drive towards a 'social conscience'. There's an unforgettable scene of McGoohan being driven to hospital with the villagers running behind chanting "Unmutual! Unmutual!"

Whose side were The Village jailers on? No one knew. But at the height of the Cold War it made gripping TV, and was in fact based on writer George Markstein's knowledge of real-life "retirement homes" for spies. It was worthy of Franz Kafka, whoever he played for.

Number Six constantly confounded his captors. Where others buckled he declared: "I will not be pushed, filed, stamped, indexed, briefed, debriefed or numbered. My life is my own. I resigned." McGoohan barked out short clipped sentences looking angrier by the minute. He kept himself occupied working out in a self-made gym in the woods, with pull ups on a tree, a punch bag and periodic fist fights with Village heavies.

He retained his essential human dignity even though the Village bar had only alcohol-free drinks and there was no nightlife, thanks to the evening curfews. As for sex, the succession of busty babes in '60s bras and Breton T-shirts who tried to gain the confidence of Number Six all turned out to be working for Number Two. Number Six even escaped with a tasty Eastern European bird called Nadia to London, only to discover that he was really back in The Village and the chimes of Big Ben were taped.

Yet Number Six never cracked, even though he must have felt more disorientated than Liam Gallagher after a night out in the West End. Once Number Two shipped in a double of Number Six and tried to convince McGoohan that he was really Number 12, bought in to help crack the sanity of Number Six. In another episode Number Six's mind was put into the body of another man using Professor Seltzman's revolutionary mind-swapping technique. They tried to convince him that he'd had a lobotomy by faking the operation and giving him more drugs than even Will Self could handle. It didn't fool him though. During his public confession he announced: "You still have a chance. You can still salvage your right to be individuals, your rights to truth and free thought."

Actually The Village did have good drugs going for it. In an early attempt at Virtual Reality they pumped Number Six full of chemicals and convinced him he

Number Six never cracked, even though he must have felt more disorientated than Liam Gallagher after a night out in the West End.

was in the spaghetti western town of Harmony, having resigned as Sheriff. Number Two explains the plan: "Fill him with hallucinatory drugs, put him in a dangerous environment, talk to him through microphones. Give him love. Take it away. Isolate him, make him kill, then face him with death. He'll crack. Break him even in his mind and the rest will be easy." It wasn't.

Number Six defeated a succession of Number Twos, most notably Patrick Cargill's paranoid sadist in 'Hammer into Anvil'. Number Six was disgusted after seeing a young woman forced into suicide and sought vengeance. Through laying a trail of false messages, McGoohan convinced Number Two that Number Six was a plant. There's a memorable confrontation in the dome where McGoohan tells a broken Number Two to report himself. He announces: "You've destroyed yourself. A character flaw, you were afraid of your masters."

Number Six was afraid of no one. Upon arrival in The Village he announced: "Unlike many of you who have accepted your imprisonment and will die here like cabbages I intend to discover who are the prisoners and who are the warders."

And he did, returning to London in the final episode 'Fall Out', a classic piece of '60s TV which featured a subterranean courtroom, cycling frogmen, a room on the back of a lorry and some bizarre renditions of 'Dem Dry Bones', suggesting that McGoohan and co had been at The Village's medical cabinet. And why not? After 17 episodes of absolute paranoia a man needs a little sedation.

Yes, Number Six was an inspiration to anyone who's ever jacked their job in – or been called "unmutual". Patrick McGoohan, Number Six, not a number but a Greatest Living Englishman.
Pete May

Roger Moore

April 1999

ROGER MOORE could have been created by some deranged music hall Dr Mengele intent on splitting the essence of Leslie Phillips and David Niven – without the critical success of either. Despite being internationally credited for being crap throughout his 50-year career, Moore's combined skills of motioning with his eyebrows and looking bemused from a variety of angles have always made common housewives want to reach for the Matey.

He remained, throughout the '60s, '70s and '80s, the quintessential dry-witted English gentleman, the best paid actor in

Even though the producers later claimed that they were scraping the bottom of the barrel in casting him, audiences adored Roger Moore's 007.

the land and one of the most famous stars in the world.

Educated at RADA, Roger was 27 and on to his second wife before he won a £100 a week contract from MGM. "It took the studio two years to realise they'd signed a real bummer and that Roger George Moore was no bloody good," he recalled. "That's what I'm going to have on my tombstone – RGM was NBG."

As film offers waned, Roger threw himself into TV work, which was gladly doling out the fat pay cheques his bookie and stomach had already become accustomed to. Starring in ITV's *Ivanhoe*, he was banned from eating too much in case his suit of armour had to be rebored.

Rog enjoyed the celebrity of TV and took roles in *The Alaskans* and *Maverick*, replacing James Garner. Food, drink and women proved to be his main weaknesses. With an established fighting weight of 12st 4lbs, he was forever having to lay off the posh buns, something he deeply resented.

Lurching on and off health kicks, he was back sinking whiskies again in 1961, claiming that he didn't like loud bangs. Shooting so many westerns had frayed his nerves and given him an ulcer: "Every time I fired a gun in *Maverick* I blinked."

But the real story was his love of a stiff drink. Even Richard Harris noted how Moore could drink him and Richard Burton under the table and still be on set bright and early. Moore noted, "Drink doesn't make me more aggressive, it makes me rather loveable actually. I order large scotches instead of small ones just for the sake of arm exercise. I've got a highly developed right arm now – the left one is for cracking peanuts."

In 1962, he took the role of Simon Templar in *The Saint*, which was to become one of the most syndicated shows in TV history. With his new-found fame came blokes wanting to knock him out in pubs. "I try to sum them up quickly," he said. "If I can give them a clear two stone, I reckon I stand a chance. Otherwise I run away. Others like John Wayne wouldn't run, but then he's got

hands the size of a German baker's."

Moore was being his usual modest self. On the set of *Shout At The Devil* in 1976, he ended up brawling with a drunken Lee Marvin who tried to punch him out for real. Moore swiftly put him on the floor by getting the first one in. "That guy is built like granite. No one will underestimate him again," said Marvin later.

Rog eventually quit *The Saint*, complaining that the characters weren't allowed to kick someone's face in or use flick knives. But he enjoyed his freedom, gambling all over the world from Mayfair to Monaco – once winning £250,000 after a night of backgammon.

Moore faced a constant battle to beat his nice guy image and the only public evidence to the contrary involved his various marriage breakups, usually to some affair or other.

In 1969, after finalising his divorce from Dorothy Squires, he married a beautiful Italian opera singer, Luisa Mattioli. They stayed married for 26 years and she bore him two sons. But stories of Roger's indiscretions soon began to surface. American actor Ed Byrnes recalled a threesome with him in 1971, where Rog remained the gentleman. "Go ahead, old boy, you first," he said to Byrnes. "No Roger, you've been so hospitable. You first." But our man was adamant. "I must insist, you first, old boy." Meanwhile, the unnamed actress,

who was sitting up naked in bed, snapped, "What the hell is wrong with you two? Are you *gay*?"

More perversely, the cleverest move of Moore's career was to get fat and drink champagne in character on *The Persuaders*, playing Lord Brett Sinclair. Starring opposite Tony Curtis, Moore was raking in £4,500 a week to Tony's £6,500. While the show's publicist claimed they were best mates, the press was filled with speculation about backstage battles and how Moore would only refer to Curtis as "that Hungarian horse fucker."

Lazy even by his standards, Moore's performance still brought him his first Bond role, in 1973's *Live And Let Die*. Even though the producers later claimed that they were scraping the bottom of the barrel in casting him, audiences adored Roger Moore's 007. After his debut,

Moore's combined skills of motioning with his eyebrows and looking bemused from a variety of angles have always made common housewives want to reach for the Matey.

Moore was set. He made a fortune and went on to appear six times as cinema's best-loved spy. Most of them were bad, but in typical Moore style, he now had the franchise's producers over a barrel. He remained aloof, accused by many – namely my old man – of reducing 007 to a kind of comic status as he shied away from Sean Connery's portrayal of Bond as a tougher, more humourless hardcase.

But then Roger Moore couldn't really do much right. If anything, it was the big bucks, his personal style and his philosophy that got him through his mostly unremarkable career. As he puts it, "I do the job, try to get along with everybody, take the money and run."
Phil Robinson

John Le Mesurier

December 1996

WILSON: "Do we really have to drag that great big gun up the hill sir? It really is an awful fag."

Mainwaring: "An awful fag! An awful fag! I'll not have the men hear you talk like that, Wilson. It's bad for morale. You sound like some public school pansy. I'd like to remind you that we're on active military service... not at one of your gin and fizz cocktail parties down the golf club. Now get the men to fall in."

Wilson: "Yes, right sir... [*strokes chin and claps hands limply*] Er, platoon would you all mind falling into three lovely lines? That would be awfully kind... yes... very nice, quick as you can please. Thank you."

Mainwaring: "Oh for goodness sake..."

When living in New York, John Lennon was once asked what he most missed about dear old Blighty. He replied, quicker than it took his wife to

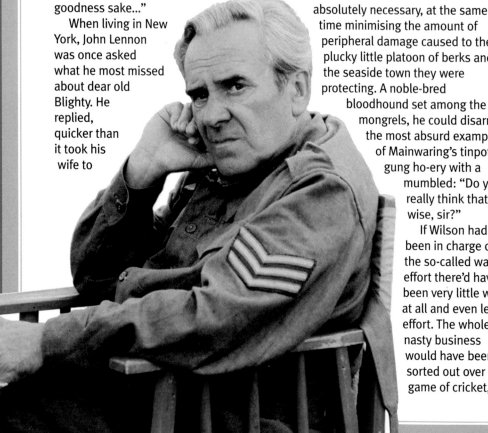

write an album, "Bath Oliver biscuits and John Le Mesurier." I don't know about Bath Oliver biscuits but John Le Mezz, the amiable dawdler best remembered for his role as Sgt Wilson in *Dad's Army*, has come to represent – with his portrayal of absent-minded High Court judges, bumbling upper middle class civil servants and feckless clergymen – everything that is quintessentially 'English'. With an acting technique consisting of nothing more than hitching up a single thick set eyebrow prior to rolling both eyes to heaven, scratching his left ear and shuffling about a bit from one foot to the other before stressing that he couldn't help thinking that everyone was over-reacting a touch, he was well up to it.

Thrust unwillingly into the maelstrom of Mainwaring's dogged war machine, he did his best to make sure his leader made no more of a fool of himself than was absolutely necessary, at the same time minimising the amount of peripheral damage caused to the plucky little platoon of berks and the seaside town they were protecting. A noble-bred bloodhound set among the mongrels, he could disarm the most absurd examples of Mainwaring's tinpot gung ho-ery with a mumbled: "Do you really think that's wise, sir?"

If Wilson had been in charge of the so-called war effort there'd have been very little war at all and even less effort. The whole nasty business would have been sorted out over a game of cricket,

weather permitting of course, settled with a few drinks down the local boozer, then sealed with an exchange of tips for the 3.30 at Goodwood.

In real life John Le Mesurier (pronounced Mezz-ur-ey) was almost identical to his screen character. He married three times, once to sitcom actress Hattie Jacques, and his third wife Joan recalls how, while he had a penchant for Jermyn Street suits, he much preferred to shamble around Kent looking like a tramp. He loved eccentrics and had an incredibly mischievous sense of humour. He would, on a whim, travel miles to visit two old ladies he knew who owned a

> ## 'All we actors require is the occasional round of applause and the odd country villa with a large swimming pool.'

parrot which he'd trained to scream "You lazy old bastard!" whenever he turned up. He knew his faults and took on other people's without a care. When reporters told him his wife was buggering off to the Riviera without him he replied, "If she chooses to have sex with a Spaniard that's her business."

Like many of us he was totally incapable around the home. When his wife went on holiday for two weeks she left his prepared meals in the freezer. Dropping round one day, Bill Pertwee, *Dad's Army* Warden Hodges, found him slumped in the living room of his huge seaside home surrounded by the entire contents of the freezer laid out on the carpet defrosting. He hadn't eaten for days as he just didn't have a clue how to turn anything on or off or plug it in in the first place.

"Although he was very dignified and reserved he had a Bohemian streak to him that surfaced at the oddest of times," recalled his wife. "He was very fond of the rock band Earth Wind and Fire and had most of their records. Of course he enjoyed traditional family gatherings but his social life centred on consorting with jazz musicians in seedy Soho pubs and visiting circus performers in their caravans.

"He was fond of a glass of beer. But he

also enjoyed smoking pot. He said it relaxed him. He smoked a joint while waiting to receive his award at the BAFTAs. He loved the idea that it was illegal."

Le Mezz's social life also extended to the races, where he knew everyone. He once shocked Bill Pertwee when they turned up at Newmarket and all the jockeys and trainers greeted Le Mezz warmly by his first name. "Everyone he met became his friend," said Bill. "The only people he couldn't stand were bores."

So he didn't hang around with any. Instead he took up with the likes of Noel Coward, who invited him to Jamaica and David Niven who had him over to Rome to help entertain some ladies during a month long boozing binge. Fred Astaire,

when he was in town, would call up Le Mezz and they'd tour London's dingiest drinking establishments til one of them passed out. And it was Le Mezz who introduced legendary piss artist Jeff Bernard to comic genius Tony Hancock. When they all shared a cab home at four in the morning Hancock scribbled his number down and handed it to Jeff saying: "Give me a call. I think you may have a little drinking problem," then promptly vomited over the seat and

He did his best to make sure his leader made no more of a fool of himself than was absolutely necessary.

passed out on Le Mezz's shoulder.

Although he much preferred to let other people get on with the business of amusing him on these nights out, he was quite prepared to give things a kick up the arse when they seemed in danger of turning dull. Once, when touring with the *Dad's Army* roadshow, someone at the BBC accidentally booked him into a gay hotel. John was most amused to discover this and without telling the rest of the

crew invited them all over one evening for drinks. When they arrived he was leaning against the bar wearing a see-through blouse and a cravat with his hands on his hips. He giggled as all the other blokes in the bar, who'd been bribed with drinks beforehand, waltzed up to him every so often and said "Ooo, hello John!" Another time when he was travelling on the coach with the cast through a quaint country village Le Mezz, bored out of his mind, pulled down a window and began bellowing obscene songs at the old codgers tottering about with their dogs.

Aside from *Dad's Army* he appeared in over 100 films including *School For Scoundrels* with Terry Thomas, *I'm Alright Jack* with Peter Sellers and *The Pink Panther* with Niven. He had little time for actors who took themselves too seriously. In a rare outburst he once blasted the idea of giving awards to fellow berks in the acting profession. "It's a farce," he said. "Absolute rubbish. Giving OBEs to people like Kenny Lynch and Harry H Corbett [*of* Steptoe and Son] and Harry Corbett [*the bloke who had his hand up Sooty's arse*]. I'm appalled. We are rogues and vagabonds the lot of us. We didn't ought to be treated in this shamefully respectable way. All we require is the occasional round of applause and the odd country villa with a large swimming pool."

He had two sons – Robin who played guitar in Rod Stewart's band in the '70s and Kim, a drummer who died of a suspected heroin overdose in Barcelona's red light district in 1991.

John himself died in 1983, leaving instructions that a very small notice should be posted in *The Times* reading: "John Le Mesurier has conked out." His last words, spoken to his wife, were "It's all been rather lovely, hasn't it?" Top gent and greatest living dead bloke, I think you'll find.
Mick Bunnage

Arthur Mullard

June 1995

ONCE ASKED to describe his average day, Arfur Mullard replied, "I'm a bit of a lazy bastard. I like to lie in bed all morning. Then I'll get up and 'ave some breakfast. A nice big fry-up. Then it's off to the park to feed the ducks. Back to the 'ouse for a plate of jellied eels. I'll spend the afternoon watching some naughty film. Then the rest of the day is spent in the boozer. I'll 'ave me fill and crawl back 'ome, pissed as a pudding. 'Alf a bottle of scotch later and I'm sleeping like a baby. Some people say to me 'you should live it up a bit, Arfur!' Well bollocks to that. I'm perfectly 'appy as I am."

Arfur Mullard has been television's favourite Fat Cockney Bloke for the good part of 25 years, best known for his role in the long-running sitcom *Yus My Dear* in which he is appropriately cast as a fat layabout with a weakness for the sauce. His catchphrase ("I'll smash yer bleedin' face in!") became an instant favourite. Weighing in at 18 stone ("An' that's just me bleedin' 'ead") with a face like a bag of chisels, more glamorous acting roles always eluded him. Not that Arfur was arsed about it. "I've never been that ambitious," he says. "Whenever the phone rings I just pick it up and say 'Ow much are you offering?' As long as the work is piss easy and it leaves me time and money for a few pints I couldn't give a tinker's."

The son of a Hoxton cable-maker, the young Arfur earned a crust as a butcher's boy and a prize-fighter before breaking into films as a stuntman and extra. It wasn't until the '60s that he began to make a name for himself, appearing in films like *The Great St Trinian's Train Robbery* and making regular television appearances with Tony Hancock and Tommy Cooper, amongst others. "I was doing all right for meself," he remembers, "but I weren't exactly overworked. Them middle-class pooves who run the telly didn't really know what to do with a geezer like me."

Then, in 1976, came *Yus My Dear* and Arfur became a household name overnight. After that came the sitcom *Rosie And Me*, in which he played a boozy old bachelor fighting a council rehousing scheme on the grounds that he didn't want to move away from the barmaid he was knocking off. The undoubted highlight of his distinguished career came in 1978: teaming up with the late great, Hylda Baker to record 'You're The One That I Want', which put Travolta/Newton-John's version firmly in the shade. A memorable appearance on *Top Of The Pops*, in which Arfur and Hylda shoehorned themselves into tight leather clobber, propelled a single into the Top 30. Suddenly Arfur found himself enjoying the perks of a pop star.

"The birds went mad for me," he recalls. "I'd get letters from these women saying that they fancied putting me kippers under their grill. Some of 'em would turn up at my flat and drag me off to the bedroom. It don't 'appen so much these days. Just as well really. I 'aven't been up to it since me 'ernia operation."

In recent years Arfur hasn't exactly been a regular on the nation's television screens but he still earns a fair whack from advertising voice-overs and

occasional appearances on celebrity quiz shows; enough to maintain the modest lifestyle to which he is accustomed. These days he lives alone in a small council house near the Arsenal football ground where he is known locally as The Duke Of Islington.

"I could have moved to 'Ollywood years ago," he says, "and become a proper film star with swimming pools and the rest. But I couldn't be bovvered. I'd rather stay where I am, sit in the pub and scratch me arse whenever I feel like it. I could be rich but I'd rather be 'appy. Nuffin' bovvers me really. When I look in the mirror, all I see is my stupid, ugly mug. It's so repulsive that

Weighing in at 18 stone ('An' that's just me bleedin' 'ead') with a face like a bag of chisels, more glamorous acting roles always eluded him.

I don't look that often. But I often think, 'You might be ugly, Arfur, but this mug has kept you in beers for years.' So I've got fuck-all to complain about, 'ave I?"

Sadly, rumours of a comeback playing the romantic lead opposite the gorgeous Joanne Whalley-Kilmer in a new BBC sitcom turned out to be a load of bollocks. Not that Arfur gives a sod.

"I look back at all I've done and I'm neither proud nor ashamed," he says. "I don't give a tupenny fuck about any of it. People say I'm unique but I dunno about that. Unique? That's what they call them geezers in the 'arems, innit?" And with that he demonstrates his comic genius by rising from the pub table and letting fly with a fart that clears the room in a trice. Arfur Mullard: top Fat Cockney Bloke.
Jon Wilde

Beryl Reid

March 1996

HAD AN AUNTIE MAUD who was the living spit of Beryl Reid. Wherever she went, she was mistaken for Britain's greatest living actress. And, for a while, she played it up to the hilt, accepting complimentary glasses of milk stout in local taverns, and wheel-barrows full of fruit and veg from impressionable greengrocers on the strength of her uncanny likeness.

However, after a couple of years of all this, the novelty began to wear itself out and the old witch would get into a right lather every time some stranger wandered up and complimented her on her acting exploits. Her patience finally ran out altogether one night when she was enjoying a quiet drink in a hotel bar. A middle-aged man approached, got down on one knee, and began to extol the virtues of her performance in the movie version of Joe Orton's *Entertaining Mr Sloane*. And with that, she rose from her bar stool, rudely turned her back and, without any further ado, farted loudly in the bloke's face.

This is the kind of behaviour that Beryl Reid herself might not completely approve of, though chances are she would see the funny side. After all, we're talking about a woman who once remarked to the *Daily Star*, "I wouldn't bat an eyelid if I learned that my best friend was having it off with a goat. I'd say 'How original, darling! What colour is it?' You see, I have a great lust for life in all its strange and wonderful permutations. Nothing really shocks me. I've seen it all and done it all in my time."

She set out her stall from the very start. Back in 1936, auditioning for her first professional acting job, a producer asked her what she did. "Everything," she replied, "absolutely everything." And so it proved. Over the last 60 years she has pretty much covered the waterfront: radio, television, theatre, panto, films, records... establishing herself in the process as the country's best-loved actress. Whether hamming it up to the nines in *The Belles of St Trinians*, out-performing Alec Guinness in *Tinker, Tailor, Soldier, Spy* and *Smiley's People*, or cracking the funnies alongside John Inman on *Blankety Blank*, Beryl Reid has never been less than bloody magnificent.

"I've always had a simple rule of thumb when approaching a part," she once said, "Once you've got the shoes right for the character, you get the walk right, and then the whole thing falls into place." With her purse-lips, goose-gog eyes and dumpling cheeks, she was never likely to be mistaken for an authentic sex siren but her many features were just what the doctor ordered when it came to character parts – comical or otherwise.

Having established herself as a household name in the '50s with radio characters like Monica The Lisping Schoolgirl, she made a successful transition to films, most notably as Richard Attenborough's raucous wife in 1962's *The Dock Brief*. Then, in 1969, she won the role that would take her to within a whisker of winning an Oscar and make her an international sensation. As the ageing lesbian in Robert Aldrich's *The Killing Of Sister George*, she turned in one of the all-time great screen performances.

However, the role was not without its difficulties. When the script required her to fondle the ample bosom of Susannah York she refused to comply, and another actress had to be drafted in to do the

honours. "It's not that I have a problem with lesbians," she later remarked, "it's just that I don't go in for all that myself. I like men too much to think about women."

Twice married and twice divorced, there have been no shortage of gentlemen callers to her little cottage on the Thames over the years, "I like them young," she once admitted, "with lots of energy. These days, people talk about 'toy boys'. But I was into toy boys before they were invented. Younger men are much keener, and that's just how I like them."

For the last 20 years she has continued to divide what remains of her energies between classic stage revivals, thumping good comedy roles and serious dramatic performances – most famously on the goggle box as the formidable Grandma in *The Secret Diary Of Adrian Mole*, and the dotty old windbag in The Comic Strip's *Didn' t You Kill My Brother?*

Over the years, her talent to amaze has never faltered for a minute. She has been equally consistent in her unwillingness to

'I wouldn't bat an eyelid if I learned that my best friend was having it off with a goat. I'd say "How original, darling! What colour is it?"'

suffer fools gladly. Prying interviewers have been known to leave her house with their ears still ringing after being told in no uncertain terms that their line of tabloid enquiry is slightly less welcome than a pork chop to a Jewish wedding. Two *Sun* reporters once turned up when her home was flooded and unwisely attempted to persuade her to stick on a pair of Wellingtons and pose for photographs. "I told them to sod off and not bother to darken my door again," she said.

Rumours that she was the award winning actress referred to as a cocaine-buyer in the trial of an Arabian playboy were dealt with equally swiftly. "I enjoy the occasional glass of brandy," she told *The Evening Standard*. "But cocaine? I wouldn't know where to put it darling."

Now in her seventies, she remains as privately prickly as she is professionally perfect. Still busier than Adam Black's trouser-zip, she throws herself into challenging roles with the same sense of wild abandonment with which she continues to devour young lads for breakfast. "Like Queen Victoria, I am not intrested in the possibility of defeat," she says. "I'm one of life's winners. I always have been and I'll remain so until they cart me off in a wooden box."

Let's hear it then for the original Beryl the Peril: the OAP whose grill the **loaded** editorial team would most like to stick their kippers under. Gawd bless her and all who sail in her.
Jon Wilde

Leonard Rossiter

October 1995

ALRIGHT, FAIR COP, Leonard Rossiter is not, technically speaking, alive and well. Indeed, he has been feeling less than rosy about the gills since the night of October 5, 1984, when his toes curled up during a stage performance of Joe Orton's *Loot.* Arguably though, the great man's work has endured better than that of any dead funny man of the century. In short, you can take your Tony Hancocks and your Charlie Chaplins and stuff them where the monkey hid the nuts because when it came to the funny stuff, Len Rossiter pissed pure gold every time. Dead as a doornail he might be, but his lifetime's work still burns with a vital flame.

"I fell into acting by accident," he once said. "It was never an ambition of mine. What I really wanted to be was a great footballer." A flamboyant outside-left, the young Rossiter earned himself the nickname 'Twinkletoes' and almost won a trial with Everton. However, football soon fell by the wayside and he was earning £8 a week as an insurance claims inspector when, at 21, he suddenly decided to launch himself as a professional actor. Throughout the '50s, he rapidly established himself as an accomplished stage performer in the classical tradition. Then, in the '60s, he broke into film and television and there was no looking back.

Possessing a face that resembled a hollowed-out turnip lit from within, romantic leads would always be out of his reach. Instead he specialised in characters that were the very last word in seediness and shiftiness. Amongst his finest '60s moments, there was the rodent-like funeral parlour director, Mr Shadrack in *Billy Liar*; the gum-booted farmer and part-time assassin in Dick Clement's underrated *Otley*; not forgetting his role in the 1967 drama, *Drums Along The Avon*, in which he played a white liberal crank who blacks up and dons a turban to do his bit for racial harmony. Not least, there was the classic *Steptoe* episode, *The Lead Man Cometh*, in which he stole the show as a devious Welshman who nicks lead off church roofs and quotes endlessly from *The Bible*.

However, it was the '70s that Rossiter's career shot into orbit. Through this decade, there was much to celebrate including his starring role in *Le Pétomane* where he excelled as the French anal impressionist who delights audiences with his ability to fart to the tune of 'La Marseillaise' and who climaxes his performances with his own version of the 21-gun salute. Even this magnificent achievement would be forever overshadowed though by Rossiter's roles in *The Fall And Rise Of Reginald Perrin* and *Rising Damp*.

Rossiter's masterful portrayal of the menopausal Reginald Iolanthe Perrin would be proof enough of his comic genius. His portrayal of Rigsby, in all his sneering, leering, snivelling glory, simply took that genius, rubber-stamped it, wrapped it up in fancy paper and left it under the Xmas tree. A combination of braggart, racist, chauvinist, reactionary and tight-fisted toerag, Rigsby was, on the face of it, the most unpleasant character ever to slouch onto the set of a situation comedy. But it was a measure of Rossiter's genius that he could make such a character irresistibly appealing without leaving you in any doubt of his unpleasantness. *Rising Damp* boasted a top-notch supporting cast including

Possessing a face that resembled a hollowed-out turnip lit from within, romantic leads would always be out of his reach.

Richard Beckinsale and Don Warrington as the two student lodgers and Frances de la Tour as the horrifying Miss Jones. But the show always belonged to Rigsby who only had to stand in a doorway, hands in pockets, fag in gob, jaw slack, sly rolling eyes lifted to the peeling ceiling, to make every last viewer fill his or her pants with uncontrollable mirth.

Like all the best British sitcoms (*Likely Lads*, *Porridge*, *Steptoe*, *Fawlty Towers*), the genius of *Rising Damp* largely rested on its achieving a perfect balance between comedy and pathos. Both these elements were flowing in abundance in the classic 1976 Xmas episode which found a forlorn Rigsby in his bedsitter with only a bottle of sherry, a lone festive cracker and his long-suffering cat Vienna

for company. The scene is touching, almost painfully sad. And yet, as ever, you know as you watch that the next wave of laughter is not too far off. And then it happens. Rigsby rises from his chair and moves to the middle of the room to stand under the mistletoe. Looking up and eyeing the mistletoe with that familiar vinegarish expression, he sighs and says, "Well, that was a complete waste of money. I can't see Sophia Loren dropping in with a hot mince pie at this hour." And you laugh along with him. You laugh like a bastard. And, as you laugh you quietly acknowledge the fact that comic genius such as this is all too rare.

Rossiter had a motto that he lived by. And this was it: "Never leave a pond until you are the biggest fish in it." When he finally pegged out in 1984, he was the biggest fish to be found in the comedy pond. And he still is for that matter. The man himself might busy himself these days pushing up daisies and counting the worms. But the comedy he created couldn't be more alive if you stuck a lighted banger up its arse.

Leonard Rossiter: one of the immortals, mate.
Jon Wilde

Ricky Tomlinson

August 1999

H E LOOKS the kind of bemused older fella who might appear on *Watchdog* after being sold cowboy double-glazing, possibly even a bit like Terry Waite after a stag weekend with Alex Higgins, Keith Richards and Bret Easton Ellis. And, despite being born in Blackpool, he is, to all intents and purposes, a Scouser.

Yet he still deserves a nod in the direction of Greatest Living Englishman because he is a bolshy, aggressive, four-eyed Northern twat and one of the best actors this country has ever produced. And he's been held in jail as a political prisoner.

You can take Olivier and all the rest of the public-school vowel-stranglers of the '30s and '40s (and Hugh Grant while you're at it), bring them back to life and let them populate the Christ-awful period dramas the BBC produce to sell to America. They're not in the Ricky Tomlinson class in any sense of the word. He has worked for Ken Loach and Alan Bleasdale and breathed life into the words of Jimmy McGovern. He is the inheritor of the tradition of

A plasterer by trade, when he left prison after two years he was blacklisted and could not get a job in the building profession.

Albert Finney, Tom Courtenay and Richard Burton (before he went all Hollywood). He can act a scene just like ringing a bell, and he has lived the life of five men.

He might be just Bobby Grant off *Brookside* or perhaps even DCI Wise in *Cracker* to some, but to about one hundred and twelve others he will always be one half of the Shrewsbury Two – which, depending upon the reliability of your sources, was either a morris dancing double act which took the West Country by storm in 1977, or the name given to Tomlinson and his co-conspirator by the media after he was arrested and then jailed for leading flying pickets during the brutal 1972 building strike. The clever money's on the latter.

A plasterer by trade, when he left prison after two years he was blacklisted and could not get a job in the building profession. And so, while harbouring a desire to play the ukulele at the end of Blackpool pier and busking in his spare time, he got an Equity card and became an actor.

Step forward Ricky Tomlinson: top actor, Scouser, genuine working class hero and poor man's Rasputin. Let's hear it for the bolshy, aggressive, four-eyed Northern twat.

At the start of the '80s he landed the role of Bobby, the, er, bolshy, aggressive, four-eyed Northern twat married to Sheila Grant, and then he was off and running. In 1982 he told the press, "This is the first Christmas I'll have worked in the last 10 years and my kids are going to have a ball. It's all looking good." And so it was, until 1988. Soon after being put in hospital by three bouncers at Stringfellow's 'Hippodrome' club (for bellowing "There's no way I am going to pay £7 for four halves of lager"), Tomlinson disappeared from the *Brookside* set and then quit, claiming the soap had turned his character into a

"villainous send up of a trade union official".

"I couldn't rest easy," he told the *News of the World*, "knowing that I was making myself into a three-times-weekly TV idiot."

He didn't hang about. By the end of the year he had begun a new double career as a theatrical agent and the landlord of a 'fashionable' wine bar in Liverpool. "I aim to have a few laughs in 1989," he said posing behind the bar of his new establishment with a half of Tetley's. Within a year he was complaining that the place was haunted. Within three, both businesses had collapsed and he was in court accused of threatening one of his former business partners (co-incidentally, the step-father of the 16-year-old girl he had started seeing). He was acquitted, but the ramifications of the collapse continued until 1996 when he was sued for £40,000 by the Midland Bank. One hell of an overdraft by any standards.

All in all, not a bad innings. And despite the bonus of a chaotic private life which makes the worst excesses of Richard Harris and Peter O'Toole look like a couple of parking violations in the same month, he has still managed to provide British film and television with some of its greatest characters. A trick which Ollie Reed, after a bright start, was never really able to perfect. Think Bobby Grant, think DCI Wise taking the piss out of Robbie Coltrane, think Jim watching Chris Evans on television in *The Royle Family* ("he's everywhere, him... He's like shit in a field") and think about him in *Riff Raff* (yes, you have to): a fat, naked, 50-year-old Scouser stood in the bath with a hat over his bollocks.

Step forward Ricky Tomlinson: top actor, Scouser, genuine working class hero and poor man's Rasputin. Let's hear it for the bolshy, aggressive, four-eyed Northern twat.
Bill Borrows

Jokers

Ronnie Barker

March 1998

T CAN'T BE MUCH OF LAUGH being fat. Climbing ladders must be an uphill battle if you're the kind of bloke who's always first in line outside the cake shop each morning. Riding the dodgems – it's no picnic if you're something of an oinker, because dodgems have a habit of tipping over if they're ridden by fat blokes. It's a well-known fact. Crawling through narrow industrial pipes is a tall order if you're a double-gutted lard bucket. Then again, if you're in the business of making people laugh, it would seem that it is a positive advantage to be something of a fat bastard.

From Fatty Arbuckle to John 'Fat Bob' Thomson, from Ollie Hardy to Johnny Vegas... the history of comedy is dominated by people with walrus bellies and arses like bay windows. Let's not beat about the bush, fat people just happen to look a lot funnier than thin types. So, before they've even opened their gobs to tell their first gag, you're already laughing like a malfunctioning cement mixer.

Of course, any roll-call of great, fat funny blokes would have to include Ronald 'Ronnie' Barker. Funny? Ye gods, he was funny! Funny as a kipper in a curly wig. Fat? Ye gods, was he fat! So fat, it's said to have taken him two trips round to get through a revolving door. So fat that he was made to pay excess baggage on his own body at airports. So fat, it's said that, when he walked down the street, he was often mistaken for a herd of buffalo fighting under an eiderdown.

He was always something of a blimp boat was Barker. Not for nothing was he nicknamed 'Chubbo' at school. But he wasn't always shit-stoppingly funny. "I was never the classroom joker," he once said. "The joking around was something that came later." He grew up with the ambition of becoming an architect. "Luckily I was rubbish at that, so I had a crack at working the theatre. That proved to be the first rung on the showbiz ladder."

He spent six years scratching a living in tatty rep, spending most of his time fighting off the advances of randy B&B landladies. "Incorrigible they were. Big women with varicose veins and lipstick smeared all over their false teeth." After that came five years treading the boards in the West End before graduating to radio and telly. He made his dent as a comic writer and performer on *That Was The Week That Was* with John Cleese and David Frost. By 1968, he'd got his own show (*The Ronnie Barker Playhouse*). Then there was no stopping the fat bastard.

Through the early '70s, he divided his time between TV sketch shows and a spot of old Willie The Shake on stage. It was like he was biding his time – waiting for the part that would make him bleeding immortal. In 1972, he turned down the part of Frank Spencer in *Some Mothers*

> ## Riding the dodgems – it's no picnic if you're something of an oinker, because dodgems have a habit of tipping over if they're ridden by fat blokes.

Do 'Ave 'Em. Just as well, really. 'Cos he'd probably have been shite in it.

Then, in 1973, he was handed a new script by sitcom writers Dick Clement and Ian La Frenais. *Porridge*, it was called. And, as soon as Barker started reading it, he knew he was wiping his arse with a silk chamois. Thus, Norman Stanley

trail appeared to go bollock-dropping cold. He'd always been a prolific comic writer, knocking out a goodly proportion of his own TV and film contraptions under the Barker-esque pseudonyms of Gerald Wiley and Jonathan Cobbold. But now, he admitted, the gags were starting to dry up. What he needed was another vehicle as vimmed-up as *Porridge* to resurrect his career. Sadly, it never checked in. By the late '80s, he was reduced to selling his talent down the river in the woeful sitcom *Clarence*, playing a short-sighted removals man in 1988.

That same year he announced his retirement. Tributes flooded in. John Cleese described him as, "the comic equivalent of dynamite". Gene Wilder

'They say Ronnie was one of the true greats of British comedy,' his mother sniffed. 'But I've never found him funny.'

remarked that he was the funniest man he'd met in his life. However, not everyone was quite so fulsome in their praise. "They say Ronnie was one of the true greats of British comedy," his mother sniffed. "But I've never found him funny. I prefer Sir Harry Secombe myself." Then there was his daughter-in-law Julia. "In all the time I've known him, he hasn't said or done a single funny thing." No pleasing some folk.

Over the last 10 years, rumours occasionally surface to the effect that Barker is about to make a TV comeback. But these have all come to nowt. Sadly – because at his very best, Ronnie Barker was one of those comedians who could be unnaturally funny. If proof is needed, just consider that Kenny Dalglish lists him as his favourite comedian of all time. Let's face it – if anyone can make that miserable twat crack a grin, then they must be on to something.

Jon Wilde

Fletcher was brought, conniving and wisecracking, into the world, taking up residence in Slade nick, sharing a cell with daft lad Godber (the late, great Richard Beckinsale), energies largely devoted to shirking work duties and outwitting the chief screw, played to narked perfection by Fulton Mackay.

Porridge lasted three series – every one a gold-plated coconut. It turned Barker into one of Britain's best-loved funny men. Through the '70s and early '80s, it seemed he could do no wrong. Except for *Going Straight*, a hapless sequel to *Porridge*, in which old lag Fletch attempted to adapt to life outside the prison walls – with chuckles at a minimum. Still, there was enough good

stuff to keep the chicken boiling in the pot. Including three mad silent films (*Picnic*, *Futtock's End* and *By The Sea*) which successfully brought Donal McGill's mucky seaside postcards to life. Then there was the *Two Ronnies*. Which, like a whole lot of '70s comedy, hasn't dated particularly well. But back in 1974, when life was such that there wasn't a great deal to laugh about, the sight of Ronnie Barker and his short-arsed sidekick Corbett dressed up in drag and acting the goat... well, that's about as gut-busting as it got.

The '80s brought *Open All Hours*, with Barker in top-notch form as lecherous old Arkwright, the stuttering shopkeeper with the glad eye for Nurse Gladys. Then the

Peter Cook

February 1995

THE YOUNGSTERS of today claim that they invented the concept of slacking – the fine art of doing bugger all. P'shaw. Peter Cook has spent his 57 years on the planet perfecting the process to the point where it can be stated categorically nobody does bugger all better. (He's on record as saying people should be given pensions when they turn 20).

Cook lists his recreations as "Gambling, gossip, and golf" in *Who's Who* and he's picky about who he'll gossip with – he won't go to dinner parties where smoking is banned. "If people think they are more interesting than a cigarette then they must be truly arrogant."

Son of the Foreign Office official who started the National Lottery in Gibraltar, Cook claimed that he was allergic to feathers, and was thus exempted from doing National Service.

At Cambridge University, he met little Dudley Moore from Dagenham and they stormed the world of showbiz with their *Beyond The Fringe* satirical show which played to packed houses of guffawing folk on both sides of the Atlantic.

Television fame came in the mid '60s, when Pete 'n' Dud's sketch series, *Not Only, But Also*, delighted the youngsters, enraged old colonels and paved the way for the likes of Monty Python. Cook's most popular character was El Wistey, a blank

In a foray into the world of rock 'n' roll, he outdrank the Rolling Stones at Ronnie Wood's wedding, attempted to get off with the bride and was driven back to London by a young heiress.

faced man in a grubby mac who sat on a park bench and talked monotonously about his friend Spotty Muldoon, the spottiest man in the world. He'd also make observations along the lines of "I saw something very interesting today. I saw a twig on the gravel and I thought it moved." Sir Arthur Streeb Greebley, on the other hand, was a man of action, and devoted his life to causes such as teaching ravens to fly underwater.

Pete 'n' Dud came up with the head to head routine in which two dim blokes, one slightly brighter than the other, converse in a public house. Then came *Derek & Clive*, two abhorrent gentlemen whose dialogues invariably ended with Cook using the word 'cunt' a great deal, whilst Moore wet his pants laughing.

His reasons for doing *Derek & Clive*

were straightforward: "It's the simple pleasure of being an evil yobbo."

After *Derek & Clive,* Dud went to Hollywood, starred in *10* with beaded-haired beauty Bo Derek and became a multi-millionaire. As Cook commented affably: "If I'd been born with a club foot and a height problem, I'd be desperate to be a star."

While Dud was living high on the hog and filming *10*, Cook played the ill-tempered manager of a dilapidated dance hall in an ITV New Wave show called *Revolver*, introducing no-hopers like The Lurkers and Eater. "That was rubbish," he'd say, after the artists had performed. In a later foray into the world of rock 'n' roll, he outdrank the Rolling Stones at Ronnie Wood's wedding, attempted to get off with the bride and was driven back to London by a young heiress.

On another occasion, Cook, a major shareholder in *Private Eye*, was due in court for an appeal by the mag against £600,000 in damages owed to the Yorkshire Ripper's wife. He spent the afternoon in the pub.

Opportunities to break into the ranks of the *Hello* set have been numerous, but every time his innate insolence and unwillingness to toe the party line hold him back. He appeared in the mid '80s big budget movie *Supergirl* and instead of hyping it up in interviews, simply commented: "She's Superman's niece or cousin. I'm not sure which."

Prior to that he was cast as a co-star in a major American sitcom, *The Two Of Us*. He hoped it would simply be a pilot for which he'd be paid top dollar, but to his dismay it became a series, which he left at the first opportunity.

Peter Cook is basically the finest cameo man in the business. When he crops up in *Comic Strip* and other movies, his first minutes on screen generally steal the show. As for the chat shows, he's unstoppable. Ever since his appearance on the *Eamonn Andrews Show* in 1968, when he told Zsa Zsa Gabor that she was "a vain, untalented non-event," he's always given good value. As soon as he lights up one of his 60 daily Superkings and slouches, all 16 stone of him, in the chair, raucous laughs, and marvellous lies (he once claimed he was a promising amateur wrestler for Devon) are guaranteed.

Hats off, then to the man who once fooled an American audience into believing that he'd been a child actor in several movies with Doris Day. Hats off to the thrice married, golf-playing claret drinker who says he's chronically afraid of being fit and in shape. "I have the same fear of fresh air. I'm always afraid when there's a lot of it around." Hats off to Peter "I don't give a toss if people say I haven't fulfilled my promise" Cook.
Andy Darling

Ken Dodd

April 1996

BY JOVE, MISSUS! What a tattifilarious day for taking your clothes off, strapping your legs round the back of your neck and saying "How's that for an oven-ready turkey?" Yes indeed! And why not inaugurate that Ken Dodd bloke into that discumknockerating hall of fame known as **loaded's** Greatest Living Englishmen while you're about it, good fellow? Ah yes, Ken Dodd. Head cook and bottle washer of Knotty Ash, King of the Diddymen, no less. Self appointed jester to the nation. And so on, until your corset bursts.

Good Ol' Doddy. Still bringing considerable pressure to bear on the nation's collective chuckle-muscle at the grand old age of 69. And, if proof were needed that the toothsome one is Britain's undisputed Master of Mirth, perhaps it's worth considering the case of Mr Alf Pegg, an OAP from Melton Mowbray who, just last year, attended a Ken Dodd show in Leicester, and was so

> **'I was once asked how I decided to become a funny man,' he says. 'The answer is that, with a face like mine, I didn't have to decide, the decision was made for me.'**

overcome with laughter that he actually shat himself.

"It must have happened half-way through the show," the gentleman in question told the *Daily Mail*. "But I was laughing so much at Doddy's jokes that I didn't realise until just before the end when I noticed that my wife was holding her nose with a woolly shawl and pointing towards my parking space. 'Alf,' she said 'I think you've crapped yourself.' And I had. Now I've seen most of England's top comedians, including Jimmy Tarbuck. And none of them have had that effect on me. Which must say something for Doddy's comic abilities."

Indeed it must. Metaphorically, of course. Doddy's been making audience's crap themselves with laughter for more than 40 years now. From the first moment, in fact, when he launched himself as a professional stand up comedian back in the early '50s. "I was once asked how I decided to become a funny man," he says. "The answer is that, with a face like mine, I didn't have to decide, the decision was made for me." Never in the history of comedy has there been a face better suited to extracting laughs from an audience. Hair that stands on end in a way that suggests he's just had an electric toothbrush rammed up his khyber. Ears like FA Cup handles. Eyes bulging like a pair of bulldog's bollocks.

Then there's his teeth – those famous choppers which resemble nothing so much as a row of vandalised tombstones. "I'm often asked," he says, "if I'd like to have my teeth changed, to make them more normal. Not on your nelly. I like being the only man alive who can eat a tomato through a tennis racket. Besides which, my teeth have become part of my act over the years. I'd be lost without them."

Throughout the '50s, touring relentlessly in the guise of Professor

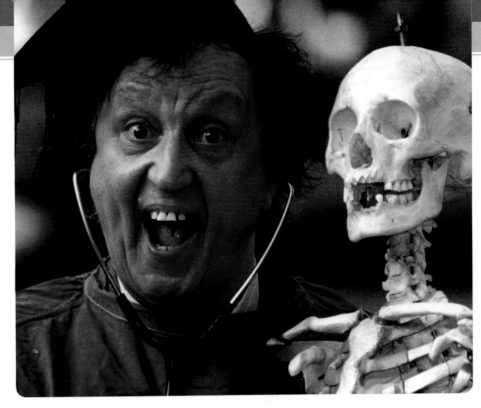

Chuckabutty ("Sausage Knotter by Royal Appointment"), he quickly established his reputation as Britain's most innovative stand-up comic. Then, in the early '60s, he made a successful transition to television with his own show, the chief feature of which was the Diddymen – a family of hunchbacked dwarfs in tall hats who were left in charge of Doddy's jam butty mines. It was sublime nonsense of the first order, and won him a huge and devoted audience. By 1964, his TV Xmas Special was pulling in close to 34 million viewers and there was no stopping him.

Even so, Doddy's television career was always destined to be overshadowed by

Then there's his teeth – those famous choppers which resemble nothing so much as a row of vandalised tombstones.

his live stand-up act where his comic imagination would capsize in a riot of daft gags and dotty fantasy. He became famous for the length of his performances which, as one reviewer noted, had a tendency to run over like an Indian khazi on Vindaloo Day. He won a mention in the *Guinness Book Of Records* for telling 1,500 jokes non-stop in three and a half hours, the average length of his live show. "No-one leaves until the trains have stopped running and everyone has enjoyed themselves to the full," he'd say. Not for nothing did he become known as The Patron Saint of the Taxi Driver.

Meanwhile, his obsession with comic detail made him known as The Slide Rule Comedian. Travelling 100,000 miles a year to perform at sell out shows, he would log reactions to his act on his so-called chuckle map, pinpointing which punchlines got the biggest laughs in which places. His ramshackle house in Knotty Ash provided a home for close to 15,000 books about comedy, and he was known to quote at length philosophical theories on the subject. "These philosopher chappies have plenty to say for themselves," he'd argue. "The trouble, though, with blokes like Freud and Aristotle is that they never had to play the Glasgow Empire on a Saturday night when Rangers and Celtic have both got beat."

One of his many catchphrases, "How you diddling?" took on new significance in 1989 when he was hauled up before the beak on charges of tax evasion. He was eventually acquitted but not before enduring a three-week trial which lifted the lid on the private life he'd always fiercely protected. Amongst other things, he was portrayed as a lonely recluse who hoarded close to £350,000 in shoeboxes in his attic – to cover himself in the event of civil war.

The public exposure left him feeling "stripped bare", but hardly caused a dent in his popularity. In fact, having given Johnny Taxman the bum's rush, Doddy emerged from court as a national hero. And the whole unfortunate saga only served to revive his career once again. Having fallen arse-over-appetite into unfashionability through the '80s with the rise of the Alternative Comedy brigade, the '90s saw him acclaimed once again as the undisputed guv'nor of the art of chuckle-making. "Fashions come and go," he reasons, "but good comedy is always good comedy. And laughter is the same thing it's always been. It's a noise that comes out of a hole in your head. Anywhere else and you know you're in trouble."

Still waving his tickling-stick about like a man possessed after all these years. Causing arses to quake with mirth wherever he treads. Yes siree! Spit on the deck, call the cat a bastard and let's hear it one more time for Ol' Doddy – the funniest fucker in all of Christendom.

Jon Wilde

LONDON PALLADIUM

HOW TICKLED I AM!

Sid James

September 1994

THERE WAS MUCH to admire about the late, great Sidney James. For starters, there was his superb comic timing, a natural talent bordering on genius that would make the current generation of mirth-makers (Lee Evans, Jo Brand, Jack Dee) look like rotten pub turns in comparison.

Then there was Sid's face, once seen never forgotten, permanently pasted with a lovely lecherous leer, and memorably described by Hattie Jacques as having "the general appearance of an ancient and dissipated walnut." However, the first thing that invariably comes to mind when

Sid's face, once seen never forgotten... permanently pasted with a lovely lecherous leer.

Sid's name is evoked is his legendary 'yuk-yuk' laugh, a feature that resembled either a gurgling drain or an untrustworthy cement mixer. In comic terms, it was the kind of laugh that was worth a million of Chaplin's funny walks and at least as many of Rowan Atkinson's rubber faces.

This contagious laugh served Sid well over the course of a showbiz career that spanned four decades. He arrived in Britain from his native South Africa after the Second World War, having previously earned a crust as a diamond polisher, masseur and professional middle-weight boxer. Relaunching himself as a character actor, he quickly established himself as the roguish mainstay of a long string of British movies. Among his best roles were the cheeky safecracker in *The Lavender Hill Mob* and the randy boarding house

75

keeper (opposite Two Ton Tessie O'Shea) in *Shiralee*, a greatly underrated late Ealing piece.

Sid's reputation gathered momentum with his role as the work shy wideboy in Tony Hancock's long running radio and TV series. But it was the *Carry On* movies that would finally establish him as Britain's pre-eminent comic rogue. It was with the saucy seaside postcard innuendo of the *Carry On*s that the dirtiest laugh in showbiz found its natural home. Sid's opening line in the 1960s *Carry On Constable* served as a reliable indicator of the riches that were to come. Playing the part of Sgt Frank Wilkins, he turns to Charlie Hawtrey's Constable Gorse and says: "Look in on Mrs Bottomley at Number 24. She complains of suspicious activities at the rear of her premises." If the obvious smuttiness of the line didn't get to your funny bone, you'd be sure to succumb to the magnificence of his impish leer and the inevitable chuckle that followed. In his 19 *Carry On*s, Sid provided more great comic moments that you could shake a shitty stick at: as a cockney Mark Antony in *Carry On Cleo*; as Sir Sidney Ruff Diamond in *Carry On Up The Khyber*; as Sid Boggle in *Carry On Camping*; not to mention his double role as Big Dick and Reverend

Flasher in *Carry On Dick*.

"Wherever I go," Sid once said "members of the public always stop for a chat. Without fail, they always talk to me as though they've known me all my life. They treat me like one of their own, an ordinary punter, which is exactly what I am." Off-screen, Sid had little difficulty living up to his roguish image. He

His legendary 'yuk-yuk' laugh, resembled either a gurgling drain or an untrustworthy cement mixer.

gambled to the hilt (usually unsuccessfully), drank like a fish (mostly gin) and possessed a marked weakness for what he would call the "ladies". Though married twice, he was a celebrated womaniser, numbering Barbara Windsor among his many conquests. The dogs and the gee-gees swallowed up most of his income, but it is said about Sid that he would take a bet on anything. Whilst filming the *Carry On*s, he would run a daily sweepstake based on how many minutes of film would be shot. On one

occasion, he was taking an early autumn stroll with a companion when he stopped under a tree and offered odds on which leaf would drop off first.

As he got older, that face resembled less an ancient walnut and more a dried-up prune, ensuring that he would never stop being funny even when faced with the challenge of bland *Bless This House* scripts. Even when his final curtain descended, the laughter simply refused to stop. At the age of 62, he collapsed on the opening night of a production of the stage farce *The Mating Game*, in the middle of a sketch which involved him sniffing a perfume bottle.

Assuming his collapse to be part of the show, the audience howled with mirth. Sid's heart had already given out, but the laughter just rolled on and on. The randy rascal had leered for the last time but the legend was bound to live on. Almost 20 years after his premature death, Sid James is still King of the Rogues; a bloke's bloke; the genuine gor blimey. *Jon Wilde*

Spike Milligan

April 1995

A FEW YEARS BACK, I had the privilege of observing Milligan's surreal, Scud-missile wit at close quarters. Spotting the great man outside an off-licence on the Finchley Road, I sidled up, waved a Biro under his nose and politely enquired if I might have an autograph. "Just fuck off, will you?" he barked. "And, while you're at it, you can take your Biro and stick it where Moby Dick got the old harpoon."

Cantankerous as an old fish wife and completely screwy with it, Spike Milligan has always exhibited the credentials of a tormented comic genius. He is Britain's most famous manic depressive and his frequent bouts of ill-temper are legendary. He once threatened to kill Peter Sellers with a potato peeler because his fellow Goon was playing jazz records too loudly. On another occasion, he shot a young vandal with an air rifle after catching the teenager trying to set fire to his daughter's Wendy House. That Spike had a few tiles loose on the roof has never been in doubt: equally irrefutable is his status as one of the great mirth-makers of the 20th Century.

Comic writer, comedian, poet, playwright, musician and actor: Spike has proved himself to be a top drawer virtuoso over the years. Yet, to his obvious displeasure, it is as an ex-Goon that he is most famous. He acknowledged this rank injustice in a mock self-obituary written for the *Sunday Correspondent* in 1990. "Terence Alan Milligan was born on 16 April 1918 in Ahmednagar, India. When he grew up, he wrote *The Goon Show*.

'You are a very tall man,' he said. 'There's a reason,' I said. 'I'm on a horse.'

Then he died." Launched in the early '50s, *The Goons* developed a huge cult following in the 10 years of their existence. They unquestionably transformed British comedy and influenced generations of future comics including *Monty Python*, *The Young Ones* and Vic Reeves. But *The Goons'* anarchic style of comedy has dated badly with the result that you'd be hard pushed to find anyone under the age of 50 who admits to finding it remotely amusing.

However, Spike's post-Goons career has been chock-a-block with great comic moments. With the exception of *The Running, Jumping And Standing Still* short (1960) and a brief but brilliant cameo in *The Life of Brian* (1979), his film ventures have been less than memorable, leaving television to provide a superior showcase for his cross-wire talents. In one of the great lost sitcoms of all time, 1969's *Curry & Chips*, he mischievously blacked up to play a Pakistani factory-worker. In 1982, he knocked a whole generation of so-called alternative comics into a cocked trilby with an utterly bonkers series entitled *There's A Lot Of It About*. Somewhere in between, came nine barmy series of *Q* which he rightly rates amongst his best work. From 1968's *Q1* to 1980's *Q9*, he ran rampant with sketches that succeeded in creating an entirely self-contained world in which logic and common sense had gone completely AWOL. Clean around the bend with bughouse brilliance, a comprehensive list of its highlights would cover an entire issue of this magazine. One moment in particular though leaves a lasting memory. It was whilst watching a totally dotty sketch, in which Spike played a man who laboured under the belief that he was a four-poster bed that I realised I had pissed myself laughing for the first time since watching my Auntie Enid climb out of the bath.

Further proof of his lopsided comic genius can be found between the pages of some of the 50 books that carry his name. In the latest of these, last year's *Wuthering Heights According To Spike Milligan*, he ingeniously miscasts the Heathcliff character as a Pakistani shopkeeper. Sample gag: "You are a very tall man," he said. "There's a reason," I said. "I'm on a horse." However, it is his endless volumes of autobiography that have had the most devastating effect on the collective funny-bone. The best of these is arguably 1971's *Adolf Hitler: My Part In His Downfall*, in which Spike recalls his army life from enlistment through to the historic landing at Algiers in 1943. The book contains the following description of how playing the trumpet put a strain on his groin: "Every time we did a gig, I improvised a truss. I stuffed rags into an old sock until it was packed tight. I then placed it in the predicted ruptures spot and attached it to my groin with lengths of tape and string.

This gave me a bulge in my trousers that looked like the erection of a stallion... Mother came to the rescue; she sewed on an additional length of dyed black curtain which covered the bulge but brought the jacket half way down my thighs. Embarrassed, I explained it away by saying, 'This is the latest style from America, Cab Calloway wears one'. 'He must be a cunt,' said the drummer.'"

Due to the criminal incompetence of the TV establishment, Spike has been a relative stranger to our screens these past 10 years. However, he made a triumphant TV comeback at the end of last year when receiving a Lifetime Achievement trophy at the British Comedy Awards. Successfully puncturing the solemnity of the occasion by referring to Prince Charles as a "grovelling little bastard" he proved that at the age of 76, he's as much a law unto himself as he ever was. Arise Sir Spike: still doolally after all these years.
Jon Wilde

Trevor & Simon

August 1995

AT ONE STAGE there were only two things that could brighten up Saturday morning television. One was switching it off and the other was a good pair of legs standing right in front of it.

Saturday morning telly was always trying to please all the people all of the time. Magic for adults because it kept the kids quiet for hours, but also having to appease the sophistication of the adults who were sitting behind the kids and screaming blue murder about cornflakes on the shagpile. Previous to the coming revolution, ITV's *Tiswas* had been the comedy standard bearer, boasting sexy Sally James in PVC jumpsuits, the Phantom Flan Flinger and Spit the Dog. Its wicked, anarchic comedy was a wild relief from the creatively constipated BBC's Edmonds/Chegwin dream team on *Swapshop*, who had allowed their comedy laurels to rest on a mauve dinosaur called Bangers.

Happily evolution always throws up a better model and a brighter dream. When Trevor Neil and Simon Wickson, aka Trevor and Simon, first burst into their audition, interrupting Philip 'greyhaired housewives' favourite' Schofield's patter while carrying a stuffed dog and a blackboard, darkened monolithic gods must have shuffled and grunted in anticipation way out in the comedy cosmos. After having the filth and politics

Simon: 'You know goldfish have only got a memory of 7 seconds?' Trevor: 'Who told you that?' Simon: 'Told me what?'

cut out of their act they were off, let loose on live TV. No doubt a lot of soiled pants went down on anxious producers' expenses forms.

Luckily for the Beeb they proved masters of the sketch, with classics such as 'Tim'll fix it' where Simon garbs up as Jimmy Savile while Trevor as an East End dandy villain on the lamb (intentionally looking like James Fox in *Performance*) tries to get Tim to fix it for him to get out of the country with a dodgy passport and a briefcase of 'Duane Eddies'.

Somewhere between Monty Python and Morecambe and Wise they worked sophisticated routines past the kids straight to the grown ups. One such sketch has Trevor as Wordsworth sitting at his desk trying to plumb Simon the peasant's mind to complete the sentence, "I wandered lonely as a... erm...". Simon asks if "I wandered lonely as a stick" would be correct. The sketch finished with Simon asking if it wouldn't be better if the famous stanza finished "when all at once I came across a crowd of... CROCODILES!"

The pair of them met when doing a Manchester University Christmas show in which Trevor had the part of a gag telling squirrel on a skateboard. Simon was a grocer who only sold meat pies and Vimto, his role involved him storming around the stage shouting about both. Simon's comedy grounding for the part came from Harpenden where he used to buy suits at the local Oxfam because that's where Eric Morecambe used to dump his old clobber.

From here they toured the Manchester club circuit, moved to London and got bit parts in *Brookside* and the unmissed soap, *Albion Market*, until they were spotted at a gig by a BBC researcher and invited to an audition for *Going Live*, one of the most successful kids shows ever.

Singing Corner was perhaps one of the pair's finest creations where they dressed up as Val Doonican/Donovan cross overs and ripped into square folky hip with the kids, community workshop types as they swung their pants to folk versions of Wee Papa Girl Rappers. It got so big that they released 'Jennifer Juniper' with Donovan and promptly snuck into the charts. Further gems from the same characters included the fictitious *Swing Your Pants Zoo* album with lyrics along the lines of "We're going to swing our pants with the Elephants."

Characters proved their strongest comic point with the Essex wideboys The Sister Brothers ducking and a diving and a bobbing and a weaving. The Brothers later recorded a single in another great comedy moment. Shot against an industrial background they performed a knockabout rendition of 'I Saw Her Standing There'. It is made all the richer by their leaving the karaoke studio and cockily saying to the bloke behind the counter, "You'll see us on *Top Of The Pops* mate." He stares at them like he's heard it all before. Cue Gary Davis introducing the Sister Brothers new single as it beats Prince and Madonna to the number one spot.

Trevor and Simon never really pushed innuendo. They didn't have to. When they were really performing the comedy was multi-layered. The finest example was

Ken and Eddy Kennedy, the barbers who were later to go on to own a dry cleaners. Both on closer examination were Quentin Crisp types, professional bachelors whose sexuality would be better examined in a long Oxbridge psychology thesis. Each week celebs would pop in for some dry cleaning. The best was Sting, on whom they dropped a running gag about his duvet being too large for the machines, then ridiculing him for having stains on it. "Urrgh Sting's duvet's rotten" and "Urrgh bee Sting, buzz buzz. What's this stain?"

In the background you can hear the crew's and the presenter's guffaws as they run through a new piece. They must have heard it all in rehearsal but in the moments of sharp improvisation and smart turns of phrase they can't help themselves.

In perhaps their best sketch they dress

up as giant goldfish, a stunt later copied for VH1 adverts. Simon: "You know goldfish have only got a memory of 7 seconds?" Trevor: "Who told you that?" Simon: "Told me what?" Trevor: "What?" Simon "What?" It continues in the same vein until they swim their separate ways. Classic.

The reason Trevor and Simon were and are so good is because it is virtually impossible to make most adults laugh without a gag about a pair of musical knackers, a vicars arsehole and a small flute. Even without swearing in their gags, and despite some quite childish slapstick, they never patronised and always managed to keep our spirits up. Trevor and Simon, so young yet already Greatest Living Englishmen. We may have to create a new accolade if you keep this up.
Phil Robinson

Stanley Unwin

May 1998

COMING ON LIKE A cross between a spindly old village fete vicar and an eccentric amateur boffin working out of a shed in his back garden, 'professor' Stanley Unwin has, over 40 years, proved himself to be a word-throttling bollock-talker of the first order. As British as bicycle clips, he's Edward Lear meets Spike Milligan with the pair the worse for half of lager shandy. "To put it single, it would appear I have this poetic fundamold humourlode which somehow strikes the trigger off in the mind of the human bean who has a concept for it. Do you imagine?" See what I mean. Total tit about arse. Clearly the Clodfather of Berk. The Goons, Kenneth Williams, John Lennon, Vivian Stanshall, Monty Python and Vic and Bob all owe a debt to this mild-mannered ex-BBC sound technician who turned to showbiz in the '50s after following General Patton around with primitive recording gear during the war.

Luckily some producer overheard him testing out some new sound gear in his garbled twatspeak. "Colly Teskers. One, two, throo, form and Fido," and he was off. These days they'd have just ticked him off for doing crack on the premises.

Soon enough his eccentric brew of drivelised gibberish was in big demand. TV, Film and Radio all wanted a slice of the man who talked cobblers. Norman Wisdom cast him as the town clerk in the otherwise knackered *Press For Time*, then Disney had him up for the Chancellor in *Chitty Chitty Bang Bang* ("Yebbers! A car floaty in the heavenly. Oh yes,"). He's probably best known as the demented old berk who drives Sid James up the wall in *Carry On Regardless* ("Don't tell me to shout my cakeload, mate,"), until Kenneth Williams, playing a smug linguist, steps in to translate.

In 1960 he recorded his own album *Rotatey Diskers With Unwin* (now available on CD) before an invited audience. Addressing every subject known to man, he successfully makes a pig's ear of the lot of 'em.

With the dawn of hippydom, Stan proved himself cheaper than drugs, providing the psychedelic back-chat between the tracks on the Small Faces' *Ogden's Nut Gone Flake* album. Soon enough he'd got himself a reputation as

the king of whimsy, working with Spike Milligan, Jimmy Tarbuck, Tommy Cooper and Ken Dodd, and rolled out to bemuse punters whenever something technical needed explaining.

In 1969 he did 13 episodes of a post *Joe 90* Gerry Anderson puppet series called *Secret Service*. Unwin plays a parish priest who shrinks his gardener assistant Matthew down to a sixth of his normal size and carries him around in a suitcase, and together they arse about solving bizarre crimes. Those who've seen the show report it to be the weirdest children's telly programme ever made. Real people and puppets are thrown

together with mental camera angles and weird perspectives; the whole caboodle liberally sprinkled with Unwin's acid-addled fractured English. Not surprisingly, Lew Grade, who was unable to understand a word, told them to "stop it immediately". Stan kept himself busy doing TV and radio ads for beer, mints, honey, Pirelli car tyres and, more recently, Kiss FM and Ronnie Scott's jazz club.

He likes a bit of jazz music, does Stan. Something he had in common with his old pal Bertrand Russell, top philosopher and a right old sourpuss by all accounts. In fact Stan reckons a lot of jazz

> ## As British as bicycle clips, he's Edward Lear meets Spike Milligan with the pair the worse for half of lager shandy.

musicians understand what he's on about better than he does. As a treat he wrote an entire history of music for them.

"The free form emerged in the '70s with a frenetty metzoff. It made bebop a languid sound of light Sunday orchestral by parison. Though not quite cuffalo teedy sound with two ploplumpers with the vicar, oh no. However all this, the '60s pewkered forth a farrago of perslodes in the musey-world. Beatloaders of Polly Carton, who with Lennontones gabe forth Leverpuddly tunes of joy with Ringold or drummage: The Rollystokers expressy fine hapload with Jagloads of mike in the lebbers swing 'n' jump huffalodown the stage and Willy Wymold of course lead guitar and plucky, the King, Elvy Presloaders, bent kneeclabber all rocky jailhouses too. In the sunshine of your snarl. Deep Joy."

In a rare, intelligible episode, he

With the dawn of hippydom, Stan proved himself cheaper than drugs, providing the psychedelic back-chat between the tracks on the Small Faces' *Ogden's Nut Gone Flake* album.

declared, "I love England. I love the word English and I love and believe in English, even though I play around with it." The "abstragger" elements which came together to make Unwinese are highly unlikely. They included having a finger blown off by electricity ("ruined me as a violinist"), a father who was a practical joker and compulsive gambler, and a mother who was a bit of a malaproper. She probably started little Stan off on his wobbly way wordwise by declaring once, "I fallopped in front of a tram and grazed my knee-clabbers." His passions, he says, are communication, language ("rhymiscan with brain usage"), comic theory and the "philosoftly" of life. He's keen on the ladies too. "Ah yes, it is a beauty to the eyebold of the symmetry of the sweet protrudey female booser. Which is a lot better than saying 'large round protrudey titty-lodes', I think."

Unwin's humour is as rich as caviar. Small doses only. Not everyone can be bothered. "My wife prefers Tommy Cooper," he says.

The secret with Unwinese, according to Stan, is not to listen too closely. You pick up the drift without understanding the words. "It's mostly rubbish with a bit of sense behind it," he says. Still ticking over nicely at 87, he recently recorded with wacky dance band Wubble U, and there's plans for a slot on a Tyne Tees TV music show called *Dr Rock* this spring. In his spare time he relaxes with a cup Cocoaload in front of *Countdown* and *Fifteen To One*, brewing up ideas. "The brainboker is still rotating and maybe a few things will pop out if I live long enough. One thing I'd like to do before I pop off is realise the connection between instinct and reason." He'll get no help from Tarbuck on that one. Cheerfold!
Mick Bunnage

Ernie Wise

May 1999

HE IS DRIVING a taxi. Eric, drunk, is hailing his cab. It pulls up, Eric climbs in and then instantly gets out of the other side. "How much driver?" he asks. "Ten shillings," says Ernie. "OK," replies Eric, "but next time don't drive so fast." A simple enough gag but perhaps one of the most important of all the thousands in the Morecambe and Wise canon, important because it amounted to their live television comeback in 1956 after a disastrous TV debut (sample piece of prescient TV criticism for their *Running Wild* series: "What's the definition of a television? A box in which to bury Morecambe and Wise") and also allowed, by way of a cock-up with the taxi which could not be moved off the stage, for the on-screen ad libs which became their hallmark. As Jeremy Novick noted in his book *You Can't See The Join*, "that sketch made them". And how.

Morecambe and Wise were not just the Vic and Bob of their day, they were something much bigger and an

influence on all the comics that followed them (to the extent that Vic Reeves' wife threatened to leave him if he didn't stop watching them on video day and night). By common consent, Eric was the funny one and Ernie the sensible one. In actual fact, Ernie Wise re-invented the straight man for television. He did not get the job through a school careers' office: "Army, no, civil service, no... oh here's one you might be interested in, it involves you being repeatedly slapped about the face by a man in thick rimmed spectacles, taunted about your short, fat hairy legs and generally made to look ridiculous in front of a national television audience of 27 million people." "I'll take it."

But this was not an unequal relationship and as much as the short-arse seemed to depend upon the berk in the glasses for laughs, so the berk in the glasses needed the little fella to set them up. Without Ernie Wise to look perplexed and then suddenly pretend to be bad-tempered, there could never have been a "Get out of that without moving." Without Ernie Wise as the tormented playwright ("the plays what I wrote are better than anything by Oscar and Wilde") there could never have been Glenda Jackson as Cleopatra or Vanessa Redgrave as Josephine. And, crucially, without Ernie Wise there could never have been, "Do you fancy a tea, Ern?"

One sketch sums it all up perfectly. Ernie is sat up in bed writing. Eric comes in and clambers in next to him. Eric is bored and wants some attention from Ernie but he refuses to stop what he's doing. Eric, listless, tries everything; even at one point asking to swap sides. "Why?" "Because my side's cold." "Shut up will you, can't you see I'm working?" He lights his pipe and, restless, gets up and walks over to the open window in a disinterested kind of way. A police car goes past with its siren wailing. "He won't

As the short-arse seemed to depend upon the berk in the glasses for laughs, so the berk in the glasses needed the little fella to set them up.

sell many ice creams travelling at that speed," he says to no one in particular. Ernie ignores him. Genius.

Like Laurel and Hardy before them, the public accepted their innocence at face value and adored them so much that the sight of them in bed together was never considered peculiar ("No one... has ever suggested there was anything immoral in it," said Ernie once. "I wear very thick trousers, you see," explained Eric). Everybody entertained the strangely heart-warming notion, at least once, that they did actually live together in that television flat.

When Eric died on 28 May 1984, the partnership was involuntarily dissolved.

Morecambe and Wise were not just the Vic and Bob of their day, they were something much bigger and an influence on all the comics that followed them.

Ernie had been the business brain behind the partnership and it must have occurred to him that the game was up, but he wanted to enjoy solo success on Broadway (Eric and Ernie had had a taste of success in America and Ed Sullivan put them on his show several times) but he had to content himself with a short run in the West End, guest appearances and a smaller part (cue Eric's raised eyebrows and blank look to the camera) in an American sitcom. But that's immaterial. His life's work was already in the can and, despite the unforgivable slight dealt him by the BBC in 1994 when they neglected to interview him for a television tribute to Morecambe and Wise ("You would think they'd ask for my memories," was all he said), he had everything to be proud of. A life well spent.

Stand up for Ernie Wise. I am standing up. Sorry.
Bill Borrows

Jackie Wright

March 1997

THERE ARE CERTAIN comedians who are able to launch a full-scale assault on the old funny bone without so much as uttering a word. There's Tommy Cooper, for instance, who would only have to saunter out on stage to have the audience filling their pants to overflowing. Same goes for Eric Morecambe and Frankie Howerd, champion mirth-makers one and all; as sure as shit to have you hooting and hollering the moment you set eyes on them.

And then there's The Short-Arsed Slaphead from *The Benny Hill Show*, a man who was surely in a league of his own when it comes to grabbing instant laughs. You'd only have to briefly conjure up his image in your mind and, within seconds, they'd be screaming for the green van to come and drag you away to

> **'He was the funniest-looking man you ever saw,' Benny Hill once declared. There was no arguing with that.**

the nearest funny farm.

Little Jackie Wright. That was the name

he answered to. Born and raised in Belfast, he discovered his gift for comedy from a very early age. "Ever since I was able to walk and talk," he once said, "I had the ability to make people laugh. I only had to walk into a room and people would fall over with laughter. Ever since then, I've ad libbed my way through life." After leaving school, he earned a crust upholstering hansom cabs. Then, in the early 1920s, having decided that the showbiz life was for him, he upped and left for the States to play the trombone with American dance bands. "I was a half-decent musician," he recalled. "But nobody took me seriously. I'd walk out on stage with a band and people would shout, 'Hey who's the funny looking bloke?' That's why I started messing about and telling gags on stage. Because I figured that, if they were laughing at me anyway, I might as well give them something to laugh about."

By the time he reached his mid-twenties, he had started touring the American variety circuit as a tap-dancer and gag-teller. It was around this time, during a stint in Chicago, that all his hair fell out overnight. "One morning I woke up and looked in the mirror," he remembered, "and I was as bald as a billiard ball. It fell out, every last blade of it, when I was sleeping. At first I was horrified. It was only when I went on stage that I realised losing my hair was the best thing that ever happened to me. I'd whip off my titfer to reveal my bald head and the audience would fall about. That's when I started calling myself Jackie Wright, the Bald Bombshell.

Later, he returned to England. For years, he took his stand-up act around the country to little acclaim. By the mid-6os, he had started making TV appearances. But mainstream success appeared to have eluded him. Then, as chance would dance, Benny Hill was looking for a regular sidekick to beef up his one-hour TV specials. Little Jackie Wright got the nod and, from there, he was drinking milk straight from the coconut.

From the late '6os to the early '8os (at which point it was suddenly pulled from the TV schedules for 'political' reasons), *The Benny Hill Show* enjoyed an uninterrupted run at the top of the

ratings. During this time, its formula remained largely unchanged, offering a mix of innuendo-packed sketches, saucy sight gags and doggerel verses.

It would have been asking a bit much for the Little Bald Feller to upstage the show's obvious main attraction – the generous helping of gorgeous nubile girls

'It's the one thing that everyone remembers whenever my name is mentioned. Having my head slapped – that's what I'm famous for.'

decked out in suspenders and mercifully short skirts who needed only the flimsiest of excuses to parade across the screen and send temperatures soaring amongst the male population. But, more often than not, Little Jackie Wright could be relied upon to upset the odds and steal the show, lock stock and barrel, from under Benny's own misshapen nose.

Arguably though, Wright was at his side-splitting best when he appeared on screen doing absolutely nothing. Not a sausage. Bugger all. Zip. Diddly-squat. Just standing there, staring gormlessly and toothlessly into the camera as Benny repeatedly slapped his dome with the flat of his hand.

A true pro, he once said that he couldn't bear the thought of life without performing and dreaded the idea of retirement. "I'd like to go straight to heaven from the TV studio," he once remarked. Sadly, it was not to be. In 1982, he sustained a serious leg injury that made performing nigh on impossible. Subsequently, he retired to his native Belfast where he lived out the rest of his days in an old folks' home. Looking back on his career, he often said that he had only one regret. "It was a pity that fame came to me so late in life. It was only when I started making a name for myself on *The Benny Hill Show* that women started paying me any attention. By then, I was too old to do anything about it."

Cracking the funnies right up to the end, Wright finally died in 1987 at the age of 83. Among those paying tribute to his comic talents was die-hard Benny Hill fan, Clint Eastwood. "Little Jackie Wright was one of the funniest men that ever lived," said Clint. "A lot of different things make me laugh. But few things ever made me laugh harder than the sight of Benny Hill slapping the little man on his bald head."

Greatest Living Englishmen? Well alright, he might not have been English. And he's no longer in the land of the living. But if greatness can be measured by one's ability to stand still while some block smacks you on the noddle, then The Short-Arsed Slaphead from *The Benny Hill Show* was as great as it surely gets. *Jon Wilde*

Heroes

Archer out of *Scum*

August 2000

FIRST RELEASED in 1979, *Scum* taught us that there are three ways of passing time as a youth detained at Her Majesty's pleasure. One: rearrange your fellow inmates' faces using socks stuffed with snooker balls; two: get gang-raped in a greenhouse and slash your wrists; three: turn veggie, feign interest in Middle Eastern religion and rip the living piss out of the entire institution.

This last path is taken by Ben Archer, one of the shrewdest piss takers in British film history, played by Mick Ford. Serving two years for dipping his hands in the till at work, he's just told officers at his previous institution that he is Christ. And so it is that he is moved to borstal, where he meets up with budding 'daddy' Carlin (Ray Winstone).

The first thing everyone notices about Archer is that, rather than wear regulation leather boots, he somehow gets away with marching around barefoot. This, he explains, is because he objects to wearing cow-skin on principle: "I'm vegetarian and I've read the rule book. They're not having me, the bastards. I won't eat shit for anyone. I'll walk out of here on crutches but they won't have me." In fact, he's no more vegetarian than Bernard Matthews. Later he decides he is no longer Christian and announces his intention to become

a Sikh. And then a Muslim. The fact that the governor is a C of E fundamentalist plays no small part in these decisions.

His smart-arse technique of warding off the wardens also works on the more brutal of the inmates. They're more scared of Archer's eccentricities than they are of Carlin's snooker balls: "I give them this wild stare around the eyeballs and they leave me alone."

Late in the film, Archer is offered

'I give you my fucking coffee and you think you can take the piss out of me?'
Yes, he just has.

coffee and a friendly chat by the kind-hearted Officer Duke (the late Bill 'Harry

Cross' Dean). From the off, Archer rubs him up the wrong way. "All I will take from borstal is evil," he says, tucking into Duke's biscuits. But it's when he suggests the lot of the officers is no better than that of the inmates that Archer really touches a nerve. As Duke yelps: "I give you my fucking coffee and you think you can take the piss out of me?" we know the answer is yes, he just has. A class act.
Chas Newkey-Burden

Captain Birdseye

February 1999

J OAN OF ARC, Guy Fawkes, Our Lord Jesus, Gary Glitter, Captain Birdseye, Hitler. History is littered with misunderstood heroes, persecuted by society for their beliefs and their delicious battered cod. Alright, so a couple of them were hounded for little indiscretions like annexing Poland, attempting to kill James I and being a witch. But how could anyone suspect this jolly red-cheeked old gentleman with his snowy-white beard and laughing eyes? "Come aboard, children," he seems to chuckle with a cheery wink. "If you swab my mizzenmast there'll be fish fingers for tea." You don't get that sort of offer much these days. But for three glorious decades, Captain Birdseye was Sinbad,

'If you swab my mizzenmast there'll be fish fingers for tea.' You don't get that sort of offer much these days.

Father Christmas and your eccentric Uncle Ken all rolled into one and every child in the country wanted to scrub his poop-deck.

Sadly, this benevolent British institution became labelled as an evil white-slaver on a par with the Child Catcher in *Chitty Chitty Bang Bang*. This was a terrible miscarriage of justice based on the shakiest of evidence. In fact, recently released CIA files traced these filthy lies back to Quorn-botherer Linda McCartney, who spread these unfounded half-truths in a desperate bid to destabilise the Cap'n's worldwide fish empire.

We mustn't allow these groundless and frankly revolting rumours to

undermine the Captain's magnificent achievements – selfless acts which have kept leaky old England afloat ever since his bizarre face first appeared on supermarket shelves back in 1967. Captain Birdseye has been the very backbone of this sceptred isle for nigh on 30 years, peddling nutrition to the nation's youth and inventing those funny little fish-shaped cod portions you get in Little Chefs. Indeed, if you laid all the fish fingers the Captain has made end to end, they would

stretch around the world 28 times, like a horrible stinking fish motorway. That's FACT. And you sewer-minded killjoys are trying to get him locked up! Traitors.

Look, just because a kindly white-haired old seadog enjoys the company of stage-school children dressed up in sailors' outfits, that doesn't make him a pervert. He's just a wise senior citizen who knows the value of vitamin D, bracing sea

air and good old fashioned hard work. It's this twisted PC-shackled era that's to blame, not the Cap'n.

You see, Captain Birdseye grew up in a time when child-loving philanthropists like Baden Powell and Fagin were regarded as heroes, not dangerous criminals. You could leave your back door unlocked, gin was compulsory and hospitals were so empty that Barbara Windsor could mess about round the wards on roller skates. Who needed a National Health Service when good luck and prosperity were yours if you just kissed a chimney sweep? See? Simpler times.

Just because a kindly white-haired old seadog enjoys the company of stage-school children dressed up in sailors' outfits, that doesn't make him a pervert.

Thus, Captain Birdseye grew up believing that everyone should help each other – and if that meant kidnapping children and putting them to work as pirates, then so be it. They'd thank him in the end. After all, none of us wanted to go to school or the dentist, did we? Kids don't know they're born.

But then, just as the Captain was plotting his massive freezer cabinet revolution, the mini-skirt was introduced, women got the vote, homosexuality was legalised and suddenly wholesome Satanic rituals involving minors became somehow taboo. The Cap'n, however, didn't flinch. A jacktar who'd fought serpents and clubbed baby seals wasn't going to be scared off by a load of guppy-stroking nay-sayers. He grabbed a big net, caught a trolley bus to the Lena Zavaroni Memorial School for Starstruck Brats and scooped up a boatful of over-privileged panto extras. He nailed them into a crate and shipped them off to the South Seas. It's all any responsible citizen would do.

And, for a time, Birdseye's boat was an

"**My** chicken dippers. Tender chicken breast and no cheating."

Captain Birds Eye

No artificial colours, flavours or preservatives

Prepared with delicious chicken breast

Eden in the sun. Days passed in a lazy haze of fishing, swimming, fishing, quoits and fishing. Now and then a film crew would paddle past and capture the ruddy glow on the faces of the crew and a cheery thumbs-up from the Captain.

OK, so there were some teething troubles. Some children, missing the glamour of *Junior Showtime* tried to escape and were brutally slain. And alright, so he did hang their rotting cadavers from the yard-arm as a warning to the others. But while he was strict, he was fair too. If anyone wanted peas with their fish fingers, they got them. Granted, many of the children perished by cutlass and cannon during the bloody cod-wars with Findus, but the Captain could always press-gang new crews on the set of

Grange Hill, Byker Grove, or *Grooey.* Happy times.

But a combination of Wings-sponsored Chinese whispers, falling fish stocks and the rise of the crispy pancake sealed Captain Birdseye's fate; he was forcibly retired to a boating lake on the Isle of Man. Now, of course, those ads are a watery *Mad Max* pastiche with a one-eyed landlubber at the helm. What kind of message is that for kids? Christ.

Let's just remember fish fingers as they were: served up by a ruddy old fat man bobbing up and down on a tug, winking at the camera and giving the kids a double thumbs-up. All aboard.
John Perry

Bob & Terry

August 1998

"**O**H WHAT HAPPENED to you, whatever happened to me, what became of the people we used to be? Tomorrow's almost over, the day went by so fast. It's the only thing to look forward to, the past."

Oof! Cheer up, squire, it might never happen. Now don't go letting anyone tell you the early '70s were all Metal Guru and berks in stacked heels kicking cans round building sites trying to look like girls. That was the upside. The downside was knowing that the '60s had been a right old knees up and the '70s had been called in next morning to empty the ashtrays and help get the stains out of the carpet. Oh dear, oh dear. It must have been like living in East Berlin with your ageing gran, listening through the wall to West Berlin having it off with Raquel Welch. Terrible business, the early '70s.

No wonder everyone stayed in and watched telly. At least there were top sitcoms. *On The Buses* (two blokes trying to buck the system), *Steptoe And Son* (two blokes trying to buck the system), *Porridge* (two blokes trying to buck the system), *Citizen Smith* (one bloke trying

'Oh what happened to you, whatever happened to me, what became of the people we used to be?'

to buck the system on his own – that's never gonna work, that one).

Of the lot, *The Likely Lads* (two blokes trying to buck the system) was the definitive item. It got the '70s mood just right. Sharp, nostalgic, anxious for the future. Even the theme tune was a right

old bellyache. Plus, of course, it was fucking funny.

Oh yes, welcome to the world of Bob Ferris and Terry Collier. *The Likely Lads*. The Gateshead glimmer twins. Admittedly no longer as likely as they'd like to be, but still on the park. Two working class blokes, best mates, once sharing mutual interest in birds, booze and avoiding punch ups in snooker halls cut adrift in a world of impending responsibilities, nagging fiancées and vicious '70s town planners tearing down their old neighbourhood and its pub faster than they could finish their pints.

"It's like my dear old dad used to say, you're not here for long. You come in with nothing, you go out with nothing. That's why he never bothered to paper the front room," says Terry, as he and Bob watch the bulldozer knock down their local.

"Oh don't you feel a touch of nostalgia. Surely these streets have their own peculiar sort of beauty," says Bob,

watery-eyed. Terry puts his fag out, pulls up his collar and gets on his soapbox. "Working class sentiment is a working class indulgence exclusive to working class people who've cracked it through sport or rock 'n' roll... or, like yourself, moved to the Elm Bridge estate at the earliest possible opportunity."

Bob sniffs. "Well I didn't want my kids brought up round here, did I?"

The beauty was that Bob and Terry, for all their differences, were two sides of the same coin. A sort of British everybloke. They were men behaving badly 25 years too early. Or Laurel and Hardy kicking around a '70s Gateshead council estate. Just two berks squaring up to the depressing thought of growing up.

There were two series of this British sitcom masterpiece. The second, *Whatever Happened To The Likely Lads*, was by far the best. Written by Clement and La Frenais, the opening titles set the tone. Ropey footage of scruffy kids with nits chucking bricks at each other on a bombsite, Bob standing in the driveway of his new house and Terry (face like a dead fish with a fag on) hanging around in the pissing rain for a bus that never stops.

Bob Ferris and Terry Collier were played by Rodney Bewes and James Bolam. When the series starts, Bob (face like a despondent bloodhound, eternal romantic, eager to please, loyal, easily led) is on the verge of marrying and settling down to a life of cosy lower middle-class security with the dreaded Thelma – indignant, uptight, ambitious, manipulative librarian who he's been on and off with since they were nine years old. He calls her 'pet lamb' and spends half his life trying to make it up to her for

whatever terrible business Terry dropped him in the day before, and the other half trying to convince Terry that he's not become the spiritless domesticated sap Terry takes him for. Thelma hates Terry. Terry hates Thelma. Terry (racing papers, eye for the ladies, council flat, self-pity, slippers and sarcasm) is Bob's best mate and represents everything Bob's trying so hard to get away from – the birds, the

> **'It's like my dear old dad used to say, you're not here for long. You come in with nothing, you go out with nothing. That's why he never bothered to paper the front room.'**

booze etc. They haven't spoken since Terry "accidentally" joined the army five years previously. Of course they joined together, to see the world, but Bob failed the medical with flat feet. Terry spent two years in a damp nissan hut in Frankfurt.

"Oh it's alright for you," says Terry. "I missed out on the permissive society, burning your bra, edible knickers and all that. I was serving Queen and country. I'm not complaining like. I learned a lot. But what have I got to show for it. Just the malaria and the war wound."

"You haven't got malaria."

"I have. I was two years in the Mediterranean, me."

"I should have thought you'd have got webbed feet not malaria."

While readjusting to civilian life, Terry, holed up in his sister Audrey's flat, makes it his top priority to stop Bob getting hitched to Thelma. "You can't marry her, man. Even at school she was so stuck up she thought her backside was a perfume factory."

Course it turns out Terry had been married himself. Some German girl. He left her the day Germany knocked England out of the Mexico world cup.

"I had no choice. It was the humiliation, man. Some things are beyond the physical. Mind you, happiest two weeks of my life." But Bob sticks by his guns. "Don't you see, Terry. From Thelma's point of view you represent a threat. The past. The 'knocking it back' and 'putting it about'. You've both got to understand that she's the one I'm working for now. Giving up all my spare time for."

"Aye... 'cept Fridays. That's lads' night," says Terry.

"Well, yes, except Fridays."

"And Tuesday. That's darts."

"And Tuesday darts."

"What about midweek football?"

"Well obviously I'll be coming with you to the football. Can't let you go on your own, can I? But she's got the rest... except Sunday lunchtime."

"It's a life of sacrifice, Bob. I just hope she appreciates it."

The dilemma is never resolved and Bob continues to live a precarious double life of boozing with Terry, staggering home to help Thelma choose curtains and all the time wishing he could flee to some desert island and live in untrammelled ignorant bliss: "Like that chap Gaugin." "What, the astronaut?" says Terry. "No the artist. Mind you, outer space should be far enough. Another half?" says Bob. "Aye. Make it a pint. The money you're on," says Terry.

James Bolam went on to do *When The Boat Comes In*, where he played a roguish Geordie entrepreneur, and did a brief stint as Jeff Bernard in the play *Jeffrey Bernard Is Unwell*, basically a rerun of Terry. I've never seen Bewes in anything else, though he probably did some panto. Who cares? This was the pair's finest hour.
Mick Bunnage

The Brigadier from *Dr Who*

November 1996

"JENKINS, THAT CHAP with the wings. Five rounds rapid!" Only one man could have uttered this immortal line. Brigadier Alistair Gordon Lethbridge-Stewart commanding officer of UNIT, the United Nations Intelligence Taskforce, set up to rescue the world from new and unusual menaces to mankind.

The Brigadier was as much a part of *Doctor Who* as the Doctor himself, starring in most of the classic episodes. When confronted with a homicidal gargoyle in 'The Daemons', the Brigadier adopted his usual trusted policy: get the chaps to waste the blighter. Bullets were useless – as they always seemed to be

Aliens, wobbly sets, dodgy acting, the same quarry doubling as an alien planet, nothing really flummoxed the Brigadier.

when UNIT confronted extra terrestrials – and the Doctor had to be relied upon for his more subtle solutions.

Nicholas Courtney played the role with just the right mix of bombast and irony. The Brigadier deserves our recognition for an excellent pencil moustache and his strikingly British reserve in the face of numerous alien invasions. A chap goes to a good school, gets a cushy job in UNIT when the only action is a night out at the regimental ball, and then this Timelord character arrives and the Earth is under threat by everything from man-eating plastic chairs to Daemons, dinosaurs, cybermen outside St Paul's Cathedral, a robotic Loch Ness monster controlled by

Zygons and giant green maggots on Welsh hillsides.

Throughout the '70s, alongside Doctors Jon Pertwee and Tom Baker, the Brigadier would each week adopt a resigned expression and utter lines like: "I see Yates. So the Doctor was frozen

stiff at the barrow and was then revived by the freak heatwave. Benton was beaten up by invisible forces and the local white witch says she's seen the devil." Sandhurst never quite prepared a chap for events like that.

Imagine the logistical problems facing

the brigadier: he's trying to supervise a conference to prevent World War Three when Daleks and Ogrons (swarthy, low intelligence creatures, a bit like Liam Gallagher turned to fat) invade host Sir Reginald Styles' country house; or put in charge of the world's top scientists, he finds they've been transported back to medieval Britain as slave labour for a stranded Sontaran; and on top of that his scientific adviser is a clever git Timelord.

When confronted with a homicidal gargoyle in 'The Daemons', the Brigadier adopted his usual trusted policy: get the chaps to waste the blighter.

What's more, he helped save the Earth with only two men under his command. It was a man's life in UNIT, if not a very long one. The regiment seemed to consist of the Brigadier and two chaps to shout at: Captain Yates and Sergeant Benton. If you spotted any member of UNIT you didn't recognise you knew they'd be zapped in action pretty soon. Yet the Brig always kept his pecker up.

He first emerged out of a London Underground tunnel in the 1968 classic 'Web of Fear', when the entire system had been closed down not by striking drivers but marauding Yeti. (He later memorably referred to it as "the Yeti do".) The Brigadier soon established his philosophy: "That's enough diplomacy, now for some practical soldiering." Which meant if it moved blow it up and afterwards have a cup of tea.

The Brig had none of the Doctor's namby-pamby compassion for alien races. Blighters who didn't even go to public school coming here trying to invade Earth – "Let 'em have it Sergeant Benton!" Lethbridge-Stewart blew up complete underground stations in 'The Web of Fear' and 'Invasion of the Dinosaurs'. Much to the Doctor's disgust

he also blew up an entire race of Silurians. When the Zygons' spaceship explodes Tom Baker asks with a mischievous grin: "That bang big enough for you Brigadier?"

His love of big bangs was probably just the Brig letting off his frustration after having to deal with countless bolshy politicians. Throughout the numerous invasions the Brigadier was constantly fending off calls from Geneva or the Prime Minister demanding explanations – probably as to why he was employing an alien with two hearts as his scientific adviser. Under this kind of pressure it was understandable if he made the odd mistake, such as mistaking an anti-matter planet for a beach in Norfolk.

The Brigadier was less sure of how to deal with women. He primly addressed Jo (Kate Manning) as "Miss Grant" and once confessed: "Women, not really my field." But he wasn't averse to a little off-duty rumpy-pumpy. When the Doctor asked a clairvoyant professor to hold Lethbridge-Stewart's watch, he saw visions of a woman called Doris in a Brighton hotel – much to the Brigadier's embarrassment. Still, even when seeing bedroom action it's a fair bet that the Brigadier's cap and UNIT bleeper would be poised by the bed ready for a message from the Doctor.

Perhaps his greatest performance was in 'The Green Death', out on video this month. There are classic lines such as: "But Doctor it's exactly your cup of tea. This fellow's

bright green, apparently, and dead."

He manages to impress, looking smooth in flat cap and sheepskin whilst driving Jo in his sports car and wearing a pinstripe suit to deal with Global Chemicals executives. He even effortlessly mingles with early Newbury-style eco-warriors in a building called the Nuthutch, while admitting that their textured fungus is just like British beef.

And there are the usual glorious battle scenes. After pollution from Global Chemicals has caused giant mutated greet maggots to burrow out of a Welsh slag heap he blows up the mine shafts and then orders airstrikes – all useless of course.

Aliens, wobbly sets, dodgy acting, the same quarry doubling as an alien planet, nothing really flummoxed the Brigadier. Even when confronted with giant maggots made from blown-up condoms his stiff upper lip remains in place, as he exclaims: "I never thought I'd fire in anger at a dratted caterpillar."

Brigadier Alistair Gordon Lethbridge-Stewart. He was the man for all invasions, the greatest ever living English chap to order five rounds at that chap with the wings.

Pete May

Dangermouse

January 1998

"HE'S THE GREATEST! He's fantastic! Wherever there's danger, he'll be there! He's the ace! He's *amazing*! He's the strongest, he's the quickest, he's the berrrrssstt! Dangermouse! *Danger-mouse*! DANGER-MOUUUSE!"

The theme song, sung by shrieking overwrought women as the world's most dynamic cartoon mouse hurdled exploding bombs, really didn't do the 'White Wonder' justice, not by a long chalk horse. *Dangermouse* (or DM, as he was known to his closest friends, and consequently, me) was the coolest thing on television in the '80s, tiny scrabbling paws down. And yes, I am taking *Tucker's Luck* into consideration.

Sandwiched saucily on Children's ITV between *Murphy's Mob* and *Razzamatazz*, *Dangermouse* stood out like a big-eared rodent in a cage full of idiot elephants simply because it was utterly, stupidly chaotic. It seemed to have been written by the proverbial monkeys chained to typewriters who had given up on Shakespeare and just started to muck about. Plot lines were ignored, loose ends left dangling like wedding tackle in the breeze and characters completely wiped from the storyboard with a damp cloth, in the name of a few cheap gags. *Dangermouse* was simply the *Tiswas* of animation.

OK, there was a very loose framework for the programme, beginning with the psychedelic, *Yellow Submarine*-style shot of the London skyline, while, over the top an announcer intoned, "London, home of the beefeater and the costermonger, home to the pearly kings... and home to the world's greatest secret agent, Dangermouse, and his roundly incompetent sidekick, Penfold."

Cut to an aerial shot of a red pillarbox

Dangermouse stood out like a big-eared rodent in a cage full of idiot elephants simply because it was utterly, stupidly chaotic.

in Baker Street where inside, relaxing in the groovy bachelor pad, DM and Penfold would receive the latest mission from their bumbling walrus boss Colonel K. Invariably this would involve a dastardly plan by Baron Silas Greenback (DM's arch-enemy, a fat Blofeld-like toad) to take over the world by creating giant chickens, turning elephants into sugar cubes, starting a plague of Egyptian pyramids that threatens to sink London; all the obvious stuff. Dangermouse and

'He's the strongest, he's the quickest, he's the berrrrrssstt! Dangermouse! Danger-mouse! DANGER-MOUUUSE!'

Penfold would then leap into their flying yellow car ("This calls for some *fancy* driving") and zoom from under a handily hinged kerbstone to save the earth by telling a few very poor jokes.

Cosgrove Hall, the sinister animation company behind the series, must have got bored very quickly, because only a few dozen episodes in, the formula was being fucked with to such an extent that, in one episode, the whole first half of the cartoon was taken up with the narrator standing on his head, swallowing his pet goldfish ('Geraldine') and getting small change stuck up his nose. These people were mental. No wonder we all turned out so weird.

Even stranger is the fact that Dangermouse was a big hit across the pond. If ever there was a series that was unapologetically British, it was *Dangermouse*, from the pathetic Music Hall humour ("Look out, the witch doctor!", "Which doctor?" "The witch doctor. He's been away for a spell...", etc) to the Anglocentric adventures themselves (Baron Greenback tries to destroy the world with bagpipe music, a flood of lumpy school custard, faulty washing machines and a monster called

'Frankenstoat', all in one episode).

And most British of all was Dangermouse himself. Dressed in a nifty white suit, patch over one eye, he was Sherlock Holmes, Jason King and James Bond all rolled into one very 2D ball. Suave, sophisticated and unflappable, even when strapped down and having his ears stretched to twice their size, his catchphrase "Good Grrrief!" injected a healthy dose of swinging '6os pencil moustachioed Leslie Phillips-isms into the proceedings.

And then there were all the other characters: the lisping Peter Lorre vole, Professor Squawkencluck, Greenback's deeply evil pet caterpillar Nero, who only spoke in farts; Stilletto, the baron's right-hand Italian crow ("Si Barone"); and, of course, DM's loyal friend and squeaky-voiced Watson, Penfold. There have, of course, been a number of twisted perverts who have suggested that the power behind the Dangermouse throne actually lay with Penfold who, like Columbo and Clouseau before him, hid a great detective mind within the bumbling speccy hamster exterior. There really is no room for this sort of talk, and if you keep it up, I'll have to summon a policeman. Did Penfold face the giant arachnid menace in 'Aaargh! Spiders!'? Did the chubby-cheeked one foil the evil rubber raft plot in 'Alping is Snow Easy Matter'? No. I rest my case.

Basically, the whole point of *Dangermouse* was just to be rampantly silly. Thus Colonel K is described as "one time desert rat, first to climb Everest on a pogo stick, cerise belt with little gold

appliqué butterflies all over it in judo, piano-thrower extraordinaire." Bonkers. The best lines, however, came from the highly-strung narrator (voiced, along with DM, Colonel K, Nero and later, the spin-off Count Duckula, by the deeply underrated David Jason), who'd almost always end the show with the words to the effect of: "Will Dangermouse be eaten by the mechanical cat? Will Penfold be shrunk by Greenback's fiendish ray? Will Colonel K escape from the treacle machine? Will this rubbish go on *forever*? Won't someone help MEEEE!!" In one episode the narrator (whose name it later transpired was Isambard) continually interrupts the action to appeal for the return of "a handknitted balaclava for a medium sized budgerigar", explaining that "the heating's packed up and I don't want Esmeralda getting frostbite on her beak".

Best episode? That'd have to be the suspiciously named 'Ee! Tea', where Greenback brings London to a standstill when he steals the world's tea ("No tea breaks, no workers: country grinds to a halt"), sucking it into the spout of a giant teapot-shaped spaceship orbiting the moon. Eventually Dangermouse is engulfed in "an enormous tidal wave of char!"

"How did you escape?" asks Colonel K, wearily.

"I took off the lid of the teapot spaceship, popped Penfold on the top, frisbeed it towards Mayfair and then hopped on board myself," replied Dangermouse nonchalantly.

"Umm... I'm not sure that makes any sense, DM..."

Dangermouse turns to the camera, winks with his one good eye and smirks, "It IS only a cartoon, sir..."
John Perry

Danny the Drug Dealer

October 1999

BACK IN 1969, drug dealers were a nicer breed. Take Danny, the hairy, unshaven and permanently high dealer from *Withnail & I*. He has none of the slightly sinister quality of, say, the smack-dealing Mother Superior in *Trainspotting*. A master of the wide-eyed, stoned understatement, Danny is a much more cuddly supplier of illicit substances, dealing mainly through a love of herbal and chemical experimentation, a joy he wishes to share with all like-minded stoneheads.

Superbly played by Ralph Brown, Danny is as much the star of *Withnail* as Richard E Grant and Paul McGann – a kind of Howard Marks without the business plan. He doesn't appear to benefit from his dealing in any material sense. You can't imagine Danny ever getting it together to put his takings in the bank. Nor are there any drug-related drive-by shootings in Danny's world. Only when pushed by Withnail does his dark side emerge, as he threatens to give him a "dose of medicine", but generally Danny is a peace-loving hippy, always ready to calm the increasingly deranged Withnail with a measured plea of "don't get uptight, man".

He is, of course, legendary for his invention of the Camberwell Carrot, a monumental joint that could utilise up to 12 papers. But Danny was much more than just a "purveyor of rare herbs and prescribed chemicals". He was also something of a philosopher. Indeed, his whole

stoned dissertation on the end of the '60s is one of the most profound moments of the film. "Why trust one drug and not the other?" he remarks. "That's politics, that is. If you're hanging onto a rising balloon, you're presented with a difficult decision – let go before it's too late or hang on and keep getting higher, posing the question: how long can you keep a grip on the rope?"

The man Withnail refers to as a "shag sack" had an entrepreneurial bent too. Having already manufactured a bottle enabling the drunk driver to give a pure urine sample, he reveals he is going into the toy industry with his friend, Presuming Ed. Danny explains that you can now buy "a doll what pisses itself", so he plans to produce one that shits itself as well.

He also claims to have something of a legal mind – "I've studied the papers" – and he knows that the best defence when inundated with eviction notices is to put the buggers in a zip up bag and light up another Carrott. Indeed, the only thing that really worries Danny is baldness. "All

He is, of course, legendary for his invention of the Camberwell Carrot, a monumental joint that could utilise up to 12 papers.

hairdressers are in the employment of the government," he explains. "Hair are your aerials, they pick up signals from the cosmos and transmit them directly to your brain. This is the reason bald-headed men are uptight." When Withnail and Marwood return from fending off Uncle Monty in the Lake District , they discover Danny has broken into their flat and met their landlord. He tells them it was not a productive meeting, as the landlord started "coming on really bald with me".

According to *Withnail* writer Bruce Robinson, Danny is based on a real-life

Camden dealer in the '60s, who went on to make his fortune as a property developer, so perhaps his schemes did amount to something after all.

Ralph Brown's Danny cropped up again in *Wayne's World 2*, in the guise of Del Preston, veteran roadie and dealer to the stars, who recounted how he once had to go to extraordinary lengths to get M&Ms – "they had to be brown ones" – for Ozzy Osbourne. Brown then battled bald aliens in *Alien 3*, and is currently a Naboo starfighter pilot in *Star Wars Episode One: The Phantom Menace*, battling the forces of intergalactic hairlessness as personified by the bald and decidedly uptight Darth Maul.

But it's as Danny at his stoned peak that we'll always remember him, pronouncing on this and that between drags on "the most powerful grass in the western hemisphere". As Marwood points out, his mechanism may have gone, but he remains the Greatest Living English Drug Dealer ever to skin up a fat one.
Pete May

Dave from *Minder*

May 1994

THERE'S BEEN a lot of Push and Shove. Certain things have happened, on the Manor... There are a lot of Villains. A lot of Plod. A lot of Villains and a lot of Plod. The Villains want a favour off Arfur. Plod wants to bend Arfur's ear too. "I'm coming over all funny, Ray, I think I'll have to sit down."

There are Microwaves, Fridge-Freezers and Satellite Dishes, all dodgy, (given a few minor adjustments, Ray...) all stashed nicely away in Arfur's Lock-Up. And Ray is wiv a Posh bird! No. It's Terry wiv the Posh Bird, and Ray's with 'is Mum! No!!!?!! Ray's wiv his Bird who's 'A Bit Posh', and Terry's wiv 'is Mum, who's Not Very Posh At All (and happens to be Arfur's sister-in-

Dave was not 'born to be Prince Hamlet, but rather one of his attendant Lords'.

law). The Fridge-Freezers are popping dodgy toast, and the Microwaves are frying 'er indoors' budgie.

We are Confused. It's Dodgy, Dodgy, Dodgy. It's All-Too-Dodgy. Things get worse. We get more confused. Villains and Plod, Plod and Villains... Where's Arfur? Terry, Ray, they're all doing their best, giving some out-of-order Villain a right old slapping, looking after the trilby, the fawn-fur crombie, polishing the Daimler, but... it seems like everyone's in a right old muddle.

So, we go dahn those stairs. Dahn those familiar carpeted stairs. Into the gin-smelling, seedy-plush, bowels of the Winchester Club – home of rooky deals, Syrupy petty-crims, and frequently frequenting Members of the on-duty-but-just-this-once Force – to meet that Face;

that gnarled quizzical boxing glove of a face, a hieroglyph of genial puzzlement.

The bar is thick with shifty, squint-eyed Villains and Plod in Pringle cardies. They vie for Dave's attention. They vie for his grizzled ear. They don't know what's happening. Like them, we don't know. What's Happening? WE ARE CONFUSED.

Dave polishes a glass. Squints, painfully. Examines it expertly against the light. He's been here before. A hundred episodes. He knows the score. He turns, leans on the bar and growls like a perturbed bear.

"Ere... run that one past me again..."

The clouds break. WE ARE NO LONGER CONFUSED. Thanks to this quiet local hero, this reliable cautious, hermit crab of the licensed premises...

"'Ere. Arfur. Someone's been in. Wants to bend your ear abhatt somefin or annuvver."

"It's not Plod is it, Dave? I've 'ad my collar felt already today."

Dave looks at Arfur's collar. It is felt!!!?!!

It is the felt collar of the fawn fur Crombie Arfur always wears. Dave's puzzlement increases. The lines on his formidable brow become the dervish dance of a spastic spider. Dave is a good bloke. Arfur's problems are always Dave's but Dave's... are never Arfur's.

Dave exists for Arfur. Dave's role in life is to field the push petty-crims and low-lifes, the ice-cream Mafiosi and savvy-challenged Plod, that clog up the smooth machine that is Daley into Europe.

He has the loyalty of a beagle on 40 a day. Scratching, with his little stub of Dave-Chalk, at a slate of cricket-pitch dimensions, untying plot-knots and clarifying all with a shot of his leathery voice.

"Make it a large one, Dave."

Dave, never too happy, never surprised, at the 'large one' shuffles towards the spirit dispensers. He lives in a world of small measures. A recent *Minder* had him, all anoraked-up at the quayside at Dover, clutching doggedly at his plastic 'Chelsea bag'. It was the only time he'd ever been out of the Winchester. His watery eyes blinked in the raw sunlight, roped in on a brilliant scheme to buy cheap booze in

France – only two years after a million of his fellow countrymen cottoned on to the same idea. The White Cliffs visibly upsetting Dave, the idea of a mere 20 miles separating him from 'dodgy water, sawn-off toilets, and Plod with guns,' obviously doing weird things to his car-sick, middle-aged belly.

It was in this now famous episode that the flame of romance was rekindled for Arfur, and we got a shuftie at a rarely-seen, affectionate, lyric side of the solid

So, we go dahn those stairs, to meet that Face; that gnarled quizzical boxing glove of a face, a hieroglyph of genial puzzlement.

and reliable, pathologically-steady, Dave.

"You should have seen Arfur in them days. He 'ad to fight them girls off he did!!!???"

His watery, Winchester-dimmed eyes welling with pure tapwater for his old mucker, separated by years and a firm elbow on a polished bar.

Dave is happy to play second fiddle in Arfur's Pop Classic Orchestra. Dave was not "born to be Prince Hamlet, but rather

one of his attendant Lords". It is his dim Winchester awareness that essentially he is a function, a 'Chelsea bag' in the dodgy Microwave-which-wakes-you-up-with-flashing-light-and-*Waltzing-Matilda* of Life.

("Dump em Arfur. They're as hot as cakes!"

"You know young Ray's right, Arfur."

"My word is my bond, Dave. You know that.")

Stubby fingers untie the twisted shoelace of plot. The man is a quintessential Mate. We all love him because we're all down the pub, happier with this bemused bear of a man, gin, and sympathy than Arfur's Quixotic adventures round the Car Lots and Dog Tracks of that sunlit, troubling world OUTSIDETHEWINCHESTER.

Holding his plastic 'Chelsea bag' in the great little earner of Life. Fielding inept Plod. Reluctantly shuffling towards the vodka-dispenser for another 'large one'. He's seen them come, he's seen them go. He's seen Arfur in more pickles than a Branston picnic, but still they throw him into bewilderment, confusion; igniting the 'Dave-flame', a gruff, Kojak-growl, the rum and pepper gargle that belies the gentle-heart of the rough-diamond geezer, the avuncular, Mum's-the-Word, indulgent, heart-breaking NEVERLETANOLDMATE-DOWN loyalty of the genial Pub Uncle, the True Mate.

Pete Campbell

David 'Bing' Crosbie from *Brookside*

July 1994

AMIDST THE DRUG USE, murder, religious fervour and debauchery that make *Brookside* what it is today, one man stands alone. No man is an island but David 'Bing' Crosbie is a rock in the cul-de-sac of chaos. Nightclubs to the left of him, bodies to the right, Bing stands firm. He is perhaps the most perfectly realised and peerless character in British soaps. *EastEnders* cannot touch him and only *Coronation Street's* Reg Holdsworth comes anywhere close. Bing can be hilarious, but he is at heart a tragic figure. "Bring on the dancing horses," he utters in disbelief as a window cleaner and photographer bring chaos to the Crosbie household. The England he once knew is falling apart before his very eyes, but he battles on with an unstoppable

Surely it is only a matter of time before, like Robert De Niro in *Taxi Driver*, he snaps and begins to administer some real justice?

combination of ballroom dancing and daft Conservative bluster.

Bing comes from a distinguished tradition of suave English twits, eccentrics and amiable buffoons. His ancestors are David Niven, Leslie Phillips and the Major from *Fawlty Towers*. From the patched sleeves of his jacket to the cut of his moustache he is every inch the Englishman, as he wanders round *Brookside* like some colonial ambassador sent to pacify the restless native Scousers

with outmoded notions of 'luck' and 'decency'. "If you see any of the gutter press," he enthuses with more than a hint of the Dunkirk spirit in the face of unwanted attention from the press pack, "then send 'em packing with a whiff of buckshot."

The key to Crosbie's existence and the foundation of his ludicrous antics is that he has nothing to do. Retirement is no

easy ride for one so inclined to action. "Marvellous hog! Sheer unadulterated heaven," he gasped when a vintage motorbike appeared on the Close.

Whilst his wife Jean busies herself in the florist, he is at a permanent loose end. Bing is a latchkey grandad, condemned to roam the

Close, as he attempts to persuade people to attend meetings and form committees, all the while dispensing unwanted advice. "I understand your predicament, but you won't find the solution in the bottom of a glass of sherry," Bing advises his recently bereaved sister-in-law.

Whilst his heart is full of good intentions and genuine curiosity, in the Beirut-like climate of the Close he is just looking for trouble. He finds himself witness to every domestic tiff and tragedy going, including ones within his own family. "Bloody Lazarus now, is it?" he asserts sternly in disbelief at Max's back-of-the-ambulance recovery. His lethal bad timing enables him to appear just when he is least needed. What makes him such a fantastic character is that he is utterly unaware that his attempts to make Brookside Close a safer, happier place often amount to little more than comical meddling. But he is not to be trifled with. He often makes references to a military past and, once awakened, the wrath of this incredible man may be nigh on unstoppable. One cannot help but feel that Bing's time has come.

He is the perfect counterpoint to the mess of Christianity, cocaine and corruption that surrounds him. From the window of his bungalow he stares out onto a sea of troubles, armed with little more than a tweed sports jacket, his moustache and an occasional burst of unregistered wit. "Tango's a bit slapdash," says Bing to his dance partner, "one more heat and the champagne's ours."

Surely it is only a matter of time before, like Robert De Niro in *Taxi Driver*, he snaps and begins to administer some real justice? May God go with him. David Crosbie, we salute you.
Michael Holden

David Brent from *The Office*

November 2004

David Brent has become a beacon of berkdom – a tower of twerpitude that will set an example to the working man for many years to come.

T HAS BEEN CUSTOMARY to reserve the title 'Greatest Living Englishman' for individuals who laboured long and hard, whether through adversity, adulation or opprobrium to carve their name firmly into the seats of the bus shelter of our consciousness. They have achieved greatness over decades, rather than had it thrust upon them over a matter of weeks. But one man has managed, through no fault of his own, to reach such legendary status in six half-hour stints.

David Brent, the manager in this summer's BBC2 comedy series *The Office*, has become a beacon of berkdom – a tower of twerpitude that will set an example to the working man for many years to come. An example, that is, of why it's not just you that hates your job.

You might argue that Brent is unworthy of inclusion in the Greatest Living Englishman series because of his status as a fictional character. But Brent is real. He lives. Ricky Gervais, who co-wrote the series and plays the smug little bastard, said there was someone like him in every office in Britain. He's not wrong.

Brent is an oil slick in a suit. He would like you to believe he's on your side. He is the man who tells you "we're in the same boat" and talks about "teamwork" when he's earning three times what you do, plotting to load all his work onto you, stop your expenses, pay rises and overtime, and put his hand on your girlfriend's arse (but "not in that way", of course).

He's desperate to be liked, but his job as Satan's little helper makes this difficult, so he prefers to tell everyone bad jokes all the time rather than actually do the things that might make him popular, because that might involve a minuscule risk to his own position. You might argue that this makes him far from a great man. But what he has inadvertently achieved is to be applauded.

First and foremost, he has shown

Whether you are a lavatory attendant or the managing director of Kwik Save, you have people above you of no apparent talent or charm.

millions of working people throughout the land that they are not alone. A life of work is a life of suffering fools gladly. Whether you are a lavatory attendant or the managing director of Kwik Save, you have people above you of no apparent talent or charm, whose stupid words and

thoughtless deeds you must pretend to respect, honour and obey.

Like Stalin, they only got where they are through claiming the credit for the hard work of other people, and by passing the buck onto those same colleagues when things went wrong. David Brent is every bit as important a figure as a man writing a confessional column about testicular cancer or the man who invented Alcoholics Anonymous, because he shows that you have no reason to respect the people above you – he explodes the myth that your bosses know what they're doing. And remember, although there may be one of him in every office, there are millions of us. Together we will prevail. I think.

Johnny Cigarettes

Dick Dastardly

May 1995

ONE OF THE MAJOR drawbacks to growing up in the early '70s was the dreadful scarcity of top-drawer cartoons to be found on the goggle-box. Unlike the pampered puppies of the '90s (piggishly plump on a steady drip-fed diet of *Rugrats, Simpsons, Butthead* et al), we young shavers of the Curly Wurly generation had to make do with a lean cuisine largely consisting of endless re-runs of *Tom & Jerry* and the completely wretched *Scooby Doo*. Then, smack in the middle of the summer holidays of 1972, the day was miraculously saved with the debut appearance of *Wacky Races* on British screens.

In cartoon terms, *Wacky Races* was nothing short of a revelation. It was loud and lurid. It was recklessly fast-paced. It was plumb loco; totalled meatballed; as mad as a maggot. In short, it was everything a cartoon should be. Produced by the estimable Hanna-Barbera team (the so called General Motors of animation) and loosely based on the 1965 knockabout movie *Those Magnificent Men In Their Flying Machines,* each episode involved a madcap cross-country racing competition in which 11 drivers competed for the title of World's Wackiest Driver.

The drivers were a truly irresistible crew, ranging from the namby-panby Peter

Perfect in his Turbo Terrific to barmy hillbillies Luck and Blubber Bear in their Arkansas Chugabug; from the sex siren Penelope Pitstop in her Compact Pussycat to The Anthill Mob in their bulletproof Bomb. But the undisputed stars of the show were the double-dealing do-badder Dick Dastardly (A dead ringer for Peter

The bastard offspring of a three-way romp between Ronnie Kray, Basil Fawlty and Terry Thomas.

Beardsley with his ski-slope chin and village idiot grin) and his snickering canine accomplice Muttley. The plot was unchanging. Each and every week, the drivers would scrap it out in a race to the finishing-line with Dastardly and Muttley devising ever more ingenious methods of wrecking the other racing vehicles. We laughed until our arses bled.

The runaway success of *Wacky Races* led to a couple of barnstorming spin-offs. Firstly, the cliffhanging *Perils Of Penelope Pitstop* confirmed the driver of the Compact Pussycat as animation's horniest invention since Betty Boop first poured herself into a mini-skirt. Indeed, it was damn near impossible to gaze at the luscious Penelope squeezed into her clitoris-pink pantaloons without nipping around the back of the sofa for a quick one off the wrist.

Then Hanna-Barbera wisely responded to insatiable public demand and gave the great Dick Dastardly his own show. In *Dastardly And Muttley In Their Flying Machines* (AKA *Stop The Pigeon!*), animation's favourite villain truly came into his own. Again the plot was ingeniously simple. Now recast as a World War One flying ace, each episode found Dastardly under orders from a mysterious general to intercept the message of the American courier Yankee Doodle Pigeon. In this, he was hindered by the ever-untrustworthy Muttley and two hopelessly incompetent mechanics in the shape of Klunk and Zilly. Every week, the inept foursome would come a cropper, allowing the cocksure pigeon to go on his merry way, sounding a triumphant "Charge!!" on his toy bugle. Finding themselves, once again, well

Wacky Races was nothing short of a revelation... loud and lurid... mad as a maggot.

fucked and far from home, Muttley would mutter some unintelligible curse and chuckle like a lunatic whilst Dastardly would utter his immortal catch-phrase: "Drat! Double drat! And triple drat!"

At its best, the show contained whack-a-doo action sequences to rival anything in *It's A Mad Mad Mad World*. In the classic *Fur Out Furlough* episode, the hapless crew are told by The General that a month-long leave of absence awaits whoever nabs the pesky pigeon. At one point in the demented proceedings, Dastardly enterprisingly positions himself on the

wing of his ramshackle plane with an outstretched net to catch the pigeon. Determined to gum up the works, Klunk and Zilly drop a piano into the net. As Dastardly plummets to earth, he orders Muttley to take appropriate action. Not for the first time, the treacherous dog proves himself to be as much use as the Pope's testicles. Calmly positioning himself at the piano, he delivers a salvo of that infectious Sidney James laugh before bashing out a few impromptu verses of Paddy McGinty's Goat. Pure bughouse brilliance.

Unaccountably, Dastardly disappeared from our screens in the mid-'70s and, aside from occasional re-runs of *Wacky Races* on Sky, hasn't been seen since. The bastard offspring of a three-way romp between Ronnie Kray, Basil Fawlty and Terry Thomas, he is still remembered as the cartoon world's most loveable rogue. Readers are encouraged to send parcels of their own excrement direct to the Hanna-Barbera studios until they decide to do the decent thing and bring Dick D and his untrusty canine sidekick back from oblivion to TV centre-stage where they rightly belong.
Jon Wilde

Jack Duckworth

November 1994

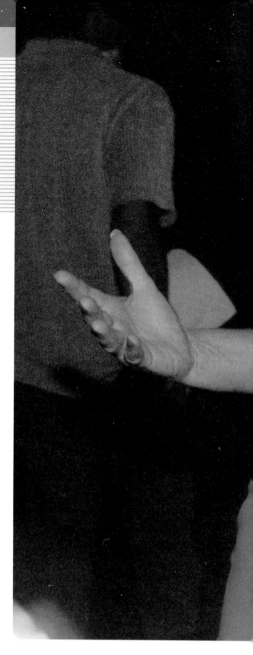

THERE WAS A PERIOD in the early '80s when *Coronation Street* seemed to have lost it big time. Everything that had made it such compulsive viewing in the first place – ingenious plot twists, rip-snorting dialogue and larger-than-life characters – seemed to be coming apart at the seams. Plot and dialogue were not insurmountable problems: nothing a fresh set of scriptwriters couldn't mend. But the sudden death of classic characters threatened to buckle the show at its knees. In the space of a few years many diehard favourites – Elsie Tanner, Len Fairclough, Albert Tatlock, Ena Sharples, Stan and Hilda Ogden – either departed, died or shuffled past their sell-by date, leaving few reasons for Joe Soap and his

pals to slump in front of the goggle box twice a week. In particular, the departure of Stan and Hilda, the soap's most loved ne'er-do-wells, created a gaping hole that seemed impossible to fill.

Then, just as the TV obituarists were sharpening their quills in readiness to ring down the Corry curtain after more than 20 glorious years, along came Jack Duckworth. Since 1979, Jack had made occasional appearances as the henpecked spouse of the formidable, bubble-permed Vera. Finally in 1983 idle Jack became a *Coronation Street* regular and almost single-handedly turned the show around and restored it to its former glories. Gravel-voiced Jack was the consummate rogue: fag in one hand, a betting slip in the other, a glad eye for the ladies and a marked preference for the boozer over the living room sofa.

From the start, he made it clear, at least when Vera was out of earshot, that no fog-horned missus of his was going to cramp his style. "You have to train 'em right," he'd advise Brian Tilsley over a mug of stout at the Rovers. "Give her a book on pigeons for a wedding present and you can't go wrong." More often than not it did go wrong for Jack and Vera would invariably catch up with him and give him what for. But it didn't stop Jack having a go and that has always seemed to be the entire point.

Over the last 10 years Jack has had numerous jobs including window cleaner, taxi-driver and market trader. More recently he has earned a crust as cellarman at the Rovers, continuing in the distinguished footsteps of Billy Walker and the great Fred Gee. Not that anything resembling work is likely to interfere with Jack's preference for propping up the bar, ogling the ladies through his Elastoplast-fastened glasses and supping at a surreptitious pint whilst complaining about his bad back. His spare time is spent squandering the "leckie money" on three-legged donkeys and attempting to corner his way out of some self-inflicted scrape.

Down the years, Jack's roguish escapades have provided us with some of television's most cherished moments. There was the time when Bet Lynch joined a video dating agency and was shown a tape of Jack himself posing as medallion man Vince St Clair. Bet responded by persuading Vera to join the agency, setting up a blind date between them, then sitting back to watch the sparks fly. There was the memorable occasion when he and Vera were nabbed by the TV detector van. Fined £100 less than expected, Jack threw an impromptu celebration booze-up only to get completely corked and plant his arse on

the telly, sending it up in smoke.

Jack has also been responsible for some of *Coronation Street*'s most dramatic moments, not least the recent occasion when he punched out his errant son, Terry, after discovering that he had sold grandson Tommy to his other grandparents. One could only assume that Jack was brassed off because he hadn't thought of it first.

Jack's finest moments though have involved run-ins with the dreaded Percy Sugden, Corry's resident nosy bastard. These include Jack chopping the top off Percy's Christmas tree to save the cost of buying one himself and, perhaps best of all, his involvement in the long-running saga of Percy's missing budgies.

Like all the best soap characters, Jack the Lad has become indistinguishable

From the start, he made it clear, at least when Vera was out of earshot, that no fog-horned missus of his was going to cramp his style.

from the actor who plays him. Bill Tarmey is cut from similar working-class cloth to Jack and, like his character, has a weakness for the fags and the sauce. In recent years, Tarmey has pursued a successful parallel career as a crooner of romantic standards. Indeed his latest collection, entitled *Time For Love*, is

released this month, but Tarmey's mainstream pop success has never threatened to overshadow his magnificent portrayal of TV's most loveable layabout.

"People seem to have a bit of trouble coming to terms with the fact that Jack Duckworth is simply the character I play," he says. "I was singing in this Merseyside club a few months back just after Jack had been seen stealing a fiver from Vera's handbag. I was halfway through a song when this old dear clambers on stage and starts telling me to give that fiver back as soon as I got home. I started trying to explain that Jack isn't real but she belted me with her handbag. Caught me smack in the bollocks she did. But that's the thing. Jack is real to people and I suppose that's the secret of his success."
Jon Wilde

George from *George and Lynne*

February 1997

O NE DAY, YOUNG MAN, all this will come to an end. You know what I mean: the beer, the birds, living the life and staying up for days before turning up for work after two hours sleep with some bird's knickers sticking out of your pocket. Yes folks! (as they like to say in the *Sun*) along with death and taxes, middle age is one of those things that's going to happen to us all. But fear not, with a role model like George to look up to age will have no sting – you'll just stop dead in your mid-thirties and tell crap jokes forever. Heaven!

There are several ways to cope with the arrival of piles, bills and a collapsing gut. You can take the traditional approach, give in gracefully, buy a pair of slippers and resign yourself to brain death on the three piece while watching the telly and

You may not fancy the life he's chosen, a constant round of topless parties and pathetic gags, but put it like that and it's a damn sight better than sitting on the allotment watching your eyesight fail.

moaning about the 'young people'. Hmm... maybe not. On the other hand you could make a right arse of yourself and fun around, Jagger-style , doing the rounds of model parties and fitness trainers until you collapse in a coma from an overdose of

Nivea. Not bad. Alternatively there is a third way, a way to age with dignity while still ripping it up like a young 'un. They call it the Georgian way.

Get a house by the river, get a boat, get a sports car, a geometrically impossible receding hair cut and, most important of all, get a top heavy bird who dresses like a cheap tart and uses the promise of a shag as an inducement to do anything from putting up shelves to lighting the barbecue. Yes, in his own way, because he's found a life that suits him and bugger the rest of 'em, George is a role model for us all.

You may not fancy the life he's chosen, a constant round of topless parties and pathetic gags, but put it like that and it's a damn sight better than sitting on the allotment watching your eyesight fail, jacking off over some increasingly semen-stiffened back issue of *Razzle*.

Naturally, George met Lynne, his

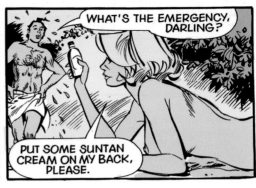

bouncy castle breasted beauty when she worked as his secretary. They have been married for an indeterminate period of time, although they first appeared in the *Sun* on 25 July 1976. Since then Lynne has miraculously got younger (see, she really is the perfect wife) while George has aged, if anything, about three years. This alone would surely qualify anyone for the title Greatest Living Englishman. Lynne doesn't work, even though they've never had children, while George runs his own business and spends his days answering calls from the missus and wondering exactly how little she'll be wearing by the time he gets home. Lynne doesn't wear a lot of clothes even when it's brass-monkey weather but every so often

George doesn't like to take a chance. "Put on something sexy and make a special dinner," he phoned up and told her once,

George spends his days answering calls from the missus and wondering how little she'll be wearing by the time he gets home.

"I've got an important client coming round for the evening." When he got home she was tarted up and knackered

after hours of slaving in the kitchen. "It's alright," he admitted, "there was no client." George just fancied a bit of top nosh and a saucy shag – oh how Lynne laughed!

George knows how to crack a crap joke. In one strip Lynne is naked (of course) and risking severe facial bruising by bouncing up and down using a skipping rope. "Tell you what," she says, handing him the rope, "I'll keep up my exercise if you do a bit of skipping."

"OK," he replies, arched single eyebrow telegraphing a joke like Roger Moore on a bad day, "but I won't need that, I'll start off by skipping my six o'clock Scotch." Ba ba boom!
Martin Deeson

The Honey Monster

May 1996

SUGAR PUFFS SALES have dramatically slumped in the Sunderland area recently. The cause of this disaster came about following an advert on the telly where the Honey Monster is seen nodding in the winner for Newcastle United and high-fiving Kevin Keegan in the post match celebrations. The fact that Honey Monster is seven foot six in his socks, covered from head to toe in yellow fur and is quite obviously not a professional footballer obviously hasn't crossed the minds of the people of Sunderland.

Still it goes to prove the power of a large honey-fixated monster with boggly eyes. You don't see people complaining when Tony the Tiger beats two blokes at beach volleyball do you? So with that in mind, and after 22 years in the business, **loaded** can bestow no higher honour than making Honey Monster the greatest living English thing this month.

Since 1974, the monster has advised

'Tell 'em about the honey, mummy,' he'd tell Henry [McGhee]. And Henry would.

us to eat the delicious golden puffed wheat called Sugar Puffs. To help him, he's been alongside such celebrities as Henry McGhee playing Honey's surrogate mother and Salford poet John Cooper Clarke as his 'mate'. The latter would wear an ill-fitting suit with a pencil tie and inform us that it was "Tummee time!" Why in God's name anyone thought of getting Cooper Clarke involved was anyone's guess.

As a child, I would insist on a box of Sugar Puffs from my mum. I knew when I was being sold something good and this large yellow fella was talking my language. Obviously I had a better grasp of vocabulary than the monster – besides uttering those immortal words, all he could do was laugh insanely and knock things over. But I loved him just the same and generally had two bowls of the stuff in the morning.

It's remarkable to note Honey's change through his career. It was just over 10 years ago when he'd come bounding into Henry McGhee's neatly laid out breakfast room, bounce to and from the walls, completely wreck everything in his path, and end up with a mouth full of Sugar Puffs. "Tell 'em about the honey, mummy," he'd tell Henry. And Henry would. Now we see him heroically rising above four defenders to meet a flighted crossed ball into the box, nut it into the top corner, and then swan off with Kevin Keegan. No one has changed so much in such a short space of time since Brian Deane of Leeds. Oh except, he was good once, and now he's bollocks. Another recent ad has him squeezing into a pair of red shorts and diving into shark infested waters to save two buxom lassies in bikinis. He'd have drowned a few years back.

Intrepid research on the monster led me to Los Angeles to track down Tim Pope, the man behind the inspirational Cure videos and currently directing the follow up to *The Crow* starring Iggy Pop. Tim's recently been offered *Alien 4*, and was first choice for *Trainspotting* if he hadn't been too busy. Ten years ago, mind you, he directed Honey Monster adverts.

"He was great cos he kind of reminded me of Robert Smith. I'd done all these Cure videos and there was like this similarity between them. They were both quite large and hairy, it was quite an easy jump for me to make," says Tim, over a stack of ribs at Barney's Beanery off

Sunset Boulevard (see, I told you we went to Los Angeles to interview him). "I was only going to do one advert and then I ended up doing a whole series of them in the end. About 12, I think... Well, he became a mate of mine. I did one where

As a child, I would insist on a box of Sugar Puffs from my mum. I knew when I was being sold something good and this large yellow fella was talking my language.

he was a rock star. Actually, when I did these adverts I innovated the idea of giving him an eyelid, he offered me a wider range of thoughts and expressions that way. We did the first advert where there were about 20 honey monsters in one too, that was a laugh."

Maybe you could explain why John Cooper Clarke was brought in?

"I didn't do those ones because he

shagged one of my ex-girlfriends."

I quickly change the subject and we chat some more about Honey Monster over a few beers to merit my air fare over there. Other stuff I discover is that Tim has still got the original box of Sugar Puffs they gave him at the advert, and also how there was a bloke called Bill who used to don the monster costume for years until Tim came along and shrunk the size of the monster. The writing was obviously on the wall for Bill, and a girl was employed in his place. Eventually I leave Tim to directing his major $70 million movie.

To get a word with the monster himself proved impossible. At his Quaker offices, they could only reveal that he's 22 years old this year, and that we should watch out, because he'll be playing a large part in the Euro '96 build up.
Pete Stanton

The Major from *Fawlty Towers*

August 1994

"**S**TRIKES, STRIKES, strikes... why do we bother, Fawlty?"

Fawlty Towers: Waiters collapse, guests are punched, fondled and ridiculed. Fawlty goes bonkers, loses his rag, screams, weeps with frustration, walks around the lobby in his vest, puts rat poison on the veal and generally turns the whole hotel into an untenable reign of chaos fuelled by a supreme comedy of errors and outrageous

'But they spread disease, Fawlty... he was over there, eating the nuts if you please!'

misunderstandings: Sybil beats up the builders, Polly throws ratatouille all over rude guests and Manuel unleashes his Siberian Hamster in the breakfast lounge.

Major Gowan, bless his freshly pressed cravat, strolls through all these mad episodes completely oblivious,

punctuating the most terrible disasters with such immortal one-liners as "Boycott got a century, Fawlty!" and "Did you know that the female gibbon gestates for seven months, Fawlty?"

He rarely becomes directly entangled in the chaos, but when he does it usually spells disaster for Basil, coming at precisely the most inopportune moment. He'll suddenly rediscover his errant memory and, like a dog with a wagging tail, blurts out crucial information, propelling Basil into a vat of boiling oil stirred by the wife.

The Major is a Rathbone-ish lady-charmer, greeting one French lady guest with a kiss and the words: "Tell me, are you by any chance... French at all?"

He struggles to remember their names and is convinced that Elsie still works at the hotel despite the fact that the waitress Polly replaced her three years previously: "That's funny," laments the Major when Fawlty puts him right, "I thought I saw her yesterday..."

But the Major is no senile loser. He's just stuck in a bygone era when women were objects to be delighted by and open doors for – you didn't have to understand them, just admire them with a chuckle as they flurried past. And swiftly back to the important men's stuff: war, cricket, good suits, fine claret. The Major is *dapper* personified.

John Cleese considered him the show's funniest character and was perplexed as to why the public preferred the tortured waiter, Manuel. But that's half the Major's appeal – if you don't get the joke, see the genius and admire the candour, it's your loss.

Fawlty loves him. He's a perennial crutch for Fawlty's archaic attitudes. The Major represents everything that Basil holds dear to his heart. He's from the old school where old habits die hard and the decline of imperialism is much lamented. Where one makes sure one is turned out impeccably in RAF tie and suit. A throwback to the good old days before the riff raff had the welfare state to send them on holiday to Torquay so they can torture hotel owners with their socialist tank tops and prole ignorance.

Each episode has a healthy smattering of Major genius, but most will remember *Basil The Rat*.

Manuel's Siberian Hamster has escaped and turned up eating the nuts in front of the Major in the bar, who nips upstairs and returns with his shotgun. Fawlty discovers him stalking around the place muttering conspiratorially "Vermin!" Fawlty rolls his eyes skywards,

convinced that the Major thinks there are Germans in the bar.

Fawlty: "We haven't got any Germans in the hotel this week, Major."

Major: "Going to shoot him, Fawlty!"

Fawlty: "Ahhh, not exactly legal

Major... killing Germans."

Major: "But they spread *disease* Fawlty... he was over there, eating the nuts if you please!"

Fawlty: (*under his breath, gingerly retrieving the gun*) "Good God! He's really gone this time."

Or maybe he was best in *The Germans*. Basil leaves a moose's head on the reception desk. Manuel finds himself in charge and begins to swagger about being behind the desk before disappearing under it, practicing his English as he goes. The Major walks into the lobby and is confronted by the moose who declares "Hello, sir, I speak Eeennngggliieeesshh very well, how arrrre yooou todayyy?"

The Major does a 360° on his heels but can find no one else in the vicinity. The moose carries on.

"It is niiiice dayyy, todayyy. I speak Eeennggllieessh, I learn it from a booook."

The Major turns his back on the moose

and does one more recce of the area during which time Manuel briefly pops his head up, sees the Major, says "Hello, Major, how are yooou today, I am verrryyy well thank youuu."

The major now enters three minutes of hilarious discourse with the moose, believing it to be an incredible new development in stuffed-beast technology. "Yes, I'm very well, old boy. Nice of you to ask. Canadian are you?" "No sir," replies Manuel the Moose. "I am from Barcelona." Bloody marvellous!

And he's enthusiastic about life, still getting over-excited about cricket, the EEC and his evening drink "Six o'clock Fawlty!" He's also eternally loyal, so much so that he even sticks up for the manager when some angry American grabs Basil by the scruff of the neck in front of the guests and points out all the things wrong with Fawlty Towers: "This is the shabbiest, worst run hotel in the whole of Eastern Europe!" exclaims

He's from the old school where old habits die hard and one makes sure one is turned out impeccably in RAF tie and suit.

the Yank. The Major rears back as if someone had called his wife a scrubber, bellowing: "Nohhhhh, I won't have that, (*big pause while the rest of the guests await his pay-off line*)... there's a place in Eastbourne."

The Major – the greatest living man in Torquay.

The Major was played by the late Ballard Berkeley. Ballard's other TV work included Father Dear Father, Are You Being Served?, Citizen Smith, The Goodies *and* Terry & June.
Tim Southwell

Michael the Geordie

June 1999

WITHIN THE fictional Linton Travel Tavern (equidistant from Norwich and London and temporary home of Alan Partridge) lives perhaps the greatest living Englishman to come out of the northeast ever. And that includes Sting. Michael the Geordie is the Tavern's handyman/barman/waiter/cleaner. His life is a mysterious cauldron of troubled army life, banal daily chores and one failed marriage, but it is his interaction with Alan which makes for some of the funniest moments of telly in this last decade.

"Ye ner... Wot aye reckon is like..." says Michael to Alan, who's just found the words 'COCK PISS PARTRIDGE' spray-painted onto his car, "if thee had themselves proper jobs, they wouldna do it ... Ya ner... a lot of 'em are frum brooken homes."

"I'm sorry..." says Alan, bemused, "that was just a noise... All I got there was 'broken homes'."

"Vandals," continues Michael undaunted. "Ye ne, meeks yu wunder what it's all aboot."

Alan looks at him bewildered: "A boot?"

So why is Michael working in a travel tavern? How long was he in the army? And why is he the only one who likes Alan? What little we do know about Michael is that he joined the forces at 17 and was taught how to "teek out"

terrorists following a spell at the Army School of Commando Training. Whether he shot anyone is unclear, but when he was stationed in Belize his anger was such that he threw a monkey into the sea after he caught it eating all his fags. He was married to a Filipino girl but that failed after she found it hard to adapt to Newcastle culture ("She's shacked up with me brother now in Sunderland"). Our only glimpse into Michael's inner psyche is when, sharing ideas with Alan on what to do with a traffic cone, he cups his hands into the shape of a tannoy ("speaker system" corrects Alan) and cries, "STOP TELLING ME WHAT TO DO." The regimental lifestyle to which Michael has been accustomed is beginning to fall apart around him.

For now, though, there will always be Alan and their conversations. Like how the monkeys of Knowsley Safari Park are only stealing wing mirrors and wiper blades because, Michael suspects, they're collecting enough parts to make a complete car and burst out of the gates. And how sausages strapped to fingers ("An' beefburgers fe parms, like") would

avoid fingerprint detection for a thief. Even discussing whether the term 'Chinky' is morally right, Michael summarises, "Oh aye, you're alright with that like because... it's a race of people... *and* it's a food."

He was married to a Filipino girl but that failed after she found it hard to adapt to Newcastle culture ('She's shacked up with me brother now in Sunderland').

Whether playing pretend shooting in the reception ("...And move and fire... move and fire...") or stealing traffic cones, their affection for each other is almost childlike. Alan likes Michael because he brings himself closer to the more rugged man he would want to be. And Michael

likes Alan simply because the DJ listens to his army stories. In fact, perhaps the only time their friendship is tested comes during a party in Alan's room. Michael arrives with half a jar of scrumpy under his arm and a steak pasty in his back pocket which he immediately sits on. Barely three minutes later he's repeating a tiresome joke concerning another guest ("He spies the cooook boook right... and he says it'll be nay use to me, man. Har har...") before turning on Alan following a dispute over whether Norwich centre should be pedestrianised ("Naa man, it's *yoos* that's got a lot to learn!"). His host tells him to leave and that's the last we see of him.

Now that Alan has his *Knowing Me, Knowing You* second series contract there'll be no more Tavern and no more Michael the Geordie. Our friend from the northeast will join Manuel from *Fawlty Towers* and Baldrick from *Blackadder* in imaginary telly land, serving breakfasts, fixing air conditioners and telling army stories. Although, of course, the last of those will just be a noise.
Pete Stanton

The Milk Tray Man

September 1999

NOT SO LONG AGO there was a man we could all look to for guidance. Someone who ate style for lunch and nerve for dinner, but always skipped pudding. A man for the people, especially the ladies. A man for his own theme tune. The Milk Tray Man.

Popular perception was that he was upper class and only went after posh birds – but not according to residents on the Truro council estate where he grew up. Born into poverty, and having been turned down for the job of postman for being too good-looking, Milk Tray Man began his career instead posting nougat through neighbours' letterboxes. At night,

his painful shyness submerged him into a fantasy world of further-away confectionery delivery. On foot at first, but as missions became more fanciful, a borrowed Austin Allegro would come in handy. Falmouth, Penzance, St Ives. On nights when the car wouldn't start, his trademark quick exit was first prompted by fear of missing the last bus home.

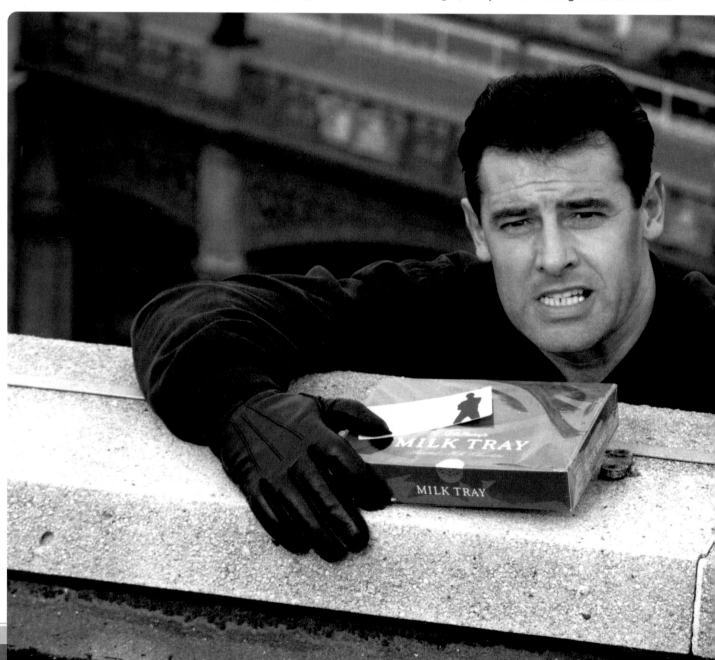

By the late 1960s, ad men at Cadbury's cast Gary Myers, an Australian model and beach bum, to bring the role to the small screen. In 1968, the now legendary trumpet parps of the Adams/Hawkshaw-penned 'Nightrider' first sounded as the cad in black dropped from a bridge onto a speeding train. Boarding at the previous station would have been out of the question.

Milk Tray Man always seemed to benefit from lax home security. He wasn't one to ignore an unlocked window leading to a bedroom of oak and moose heads. Once inside, his briefcase clicked open and a lovingly-angled box of chocs was left by the bed. Yet in less time than it took to choose between the coffee crème and the lime cordial centre, he'd vanish. Judging by her fingering of his calling card, if he had stayed the night he'd have got more than a slap-up breakfast.

But it was the 1970 Blue Grotto incident in Malta that inspired a nation of lacklustre Dereks to part with £1 for something to please the missus. Standing high on a clifftop in the noon-day sun, sweat prickling under his black polo-neck, Milk Tray Man swan-dived towards the crystal water hundreds of feet below, selling a Pele-esque dummy to a smiling shark before dispatching his confection aboard a

Milk Tray Man always seemed to benefit from lax home security. He wasn't one to ignore an unlocked window leading to a bedroom of oak and moose heads.

yacht. No time for romance – it was a diver's knife, not a rose, clenched between his teeth on the swim back to shore.

In 1972, a driving ban meant he had to outrun wolves on foot. Even though the familiar jingle had gone a bit Piggy Malone & Charlie Farley, Milk Tray Man still had enough wind in his sails to catch up with a taking-off seaplane and make a sweet-toothed deposit in its mink-lined sleeping cabin.

After a four-year absence, rumours that our hero had joined the SAS were dismissed by a 1978 incident at a snow-capped fortress near Ulan Bator, where a crinkle-faced Bedouin armed with a grapple hook and dynamite had left a box of Cadbury's finest. As he leapt onto a waiting pony like a *Scooby Doo* villain, the intruder peeled back his Mongolian hood to reveal himself as our man.

By the early '80s he'd taken to driving a speedboat down a waterfall to do a drop-off at an Austrian castle. But by 1988 such behaviour seemed old hat, and our hero was restyled to resemble the keyboard player from Level 42. Tragically, irony set in as the 'lady' handed him a Gyles Brandreth sweater to the accompaniment of a Shakatak B-side.

And what of the real Milk Tray Man now? There are conflicting reports. Some say he moved to Ghana to be nearer the cocoa plant, others insist they've seen him round Bristol on a moped delivering pizza, naturally letting himself in through an upstairs window. A symbol of yesteryear panache, a tiger who could speed-fuck for England. He's still running, still dodging bodyguards, still hanging from cable cars. And all because the lady loves Milk Tray.
Sean Vaardal

Stan Ogden & Eddie Yeats

November 1995

THERE HAVE BEEN some top-notch double-acts over the years. Bonnie and Clyde. Best and Law. Whizzer and Chips. Regan and Carter. Reeves and Mortimer. Dynamic duos the lot of them. But none of the buggers could hold a flaming candle to the double-barrelled shotgun that *Coronation Street* created when they teamed up Eddie Yeats and Stan Ogden.

There was a time in the not-so-distant past when *Coronation Street* was by far and away the best thing to be found on the goggle box. Rewind to the late '60s and early '70s and you'll find some of the finest characters ever to justify the effort of avoiding paying the licence fee. Among them were Stan and Hilda Ogden, a couple of eternal ne'er-do-wells whose endless battles against the forces of fate and common sense elevated *Coronation Street* beyond the confines of soap to a space between Ealing comedy and the best of kitchen-sink drama.

One of nature's great slackers, Stan's purpose in life seemed to begin and end with the avoidance of anything resembling hard graft. The mere mention of work was enough to make him come over all faint and he would devise ever more ingenious ways to keep out of its way. Occasionally though, a job did sneak up on him unawares and catch him with his Y-fronts down. He laboured at various times as a lorry-driver, chauffeur, coal-man, ice-cream salesman and even sculptor. But never for long. And that's just how he liked it.

Hapless bastard that he was, Stan's forte was getting into mammoth scrapes. Like, for instance, the time that his considerable girth ensured that he got stuck in a wardrobe whilst attempting an escapolgist act at the Weatherfield carnival. Or the time that he got locked up overnight in the cellar of the Rover's Return with only Albert Tatlock and 48 crates of Newton & Ridley's finest bitter for company. Top-drawer capers one and all. But, even so, you were always left with the impression that Stan would be far more deadly in the funny-bone department if he had a foil.

And so it came to pass, around Christmas 1974, that Eddie Yeats was hauled in to perk up the proceedings, having been let out on parole from Walton jail. A roly-poly (ie: extremely fat) Scouser with a heart of blancmange, Eddie was soon to be up to the kind of mischief that would make him an instant legend. Indeed, in his very first episode, he could be found cashing in on a power cut by flogging cut-price candles down at the Rovers. In a later episode, he was briefly employed as a playleader at the local school and enterprisingly kept the young 'uns busy by teaching them how to pilfer lead off the church roof. Most memorably, there was the occasion he managed to flog Annie Walker a living room carpet monogrammed in gold. So impressed was the old crone with the interlocking A and W on the imitation Axminster that she invited all the local top nobs around to

admire it. Only then was it revealed that Eddie had lifted the moth-eaten thing from the local Alhambra Weatherfield bingo hall.

In the summer of 1976, Eddie moved into the Ogdens' as a lodger. From this point on almost every episode would find Stan and Eddie embroiled in some fresh

Bad eggs and rapscallions to a man. God's own wastrels. An example to us all.

and frantic calamity. They bought a dishevelled dog called Fury and attempted to branch into the guard-dog business only to discover that Fury was actually a rabid wolf recently escaped from a private zoo. They brewed beer in Hilda's bath, planning to sell it from the back of a stolen ice-cream van, only to be nabbed by their first ever customer, a local copper who hauled them off to appear before the beak. Then there was the unforgettable saga involving Ena Sharple's bed.

Unable to afford new sleeping accommodation, Ena was insistent that she would not accept charity from neighbours. Ever willing to exercise their community spirit, Stan and Eddie hatched an elaborate plan involving breaking into Ena's and

swapping her old bed for a new one heisted from the local market. All this they somehow accomplished. The following morning, just as the old bed was being hauled off to the dump by the binmen, Eddie and Stan were enjoying a celebratory pint in the Rovers when in walks Ena to announce that some thieving sods had made off with her old mattress containing her entire life savings.

They carried on in similar vein up until the early '80s. Then, tragically, Stan was informed by his doctor that he was allergic to beer and would have to limit his elbow-bending action to orange squash. With Stan off the sauce, things would never be the same again. And, when Eddie began stepping out with a simple-minded lass called Marion, the spell was finally broken. However, just before Eddie was written out, he and Stan embarked on one last caper that captured them at their crafty, conniving best.

Having been informed by a fairground clairvoyant that she possessed a previously untapped talent for painting, Hilda took to the canvas with a vengeance. Stan and Eddie soon made off to the Rovers with one of Hilda's creations and palmed it off on the ever-gullible Annie Walker, having convinced her that it was a lost masterpiece by some primitive artist from darkest Africa. Stan and Eddie then waltzed off home, 30 quid the richer, leaving Mrs Walker to admire her invaluable acquisition. Then, picking up her reading glasses, she stopped to examine the message scrawled on the back of the canvas, "Stan and Eddie," it read, "I'm out at bingo. Your lamb chops are in the oven."

Fifteen years on, apart from Curly and Reg, *Coronation Street* is a poor imitation of its former self. Eddie (Geoffrey Hughes) earns a crust playing the token working-class pig in awful sitcoms. Stan (Bernard Youens) sadly cashed in his chips in 1984. They're gone but not forgotten. While they lasted, they were the dream of vagabonds. Bad eggs and rapscallions to a man. God's own wastrels. An example to us all.

Jon Wilde

Frank Spencer

December 1995

"**W**IZARD keep your carrots, and all that you've amassed, untie these ropes, undo this spell, I will not be harassed." (Frank Spencer – people's poet)

I was never a fan of Frank Spencer when it was all "Oooh Betty, I think I've wet myself". For the same reason I could never truly laugh at Charlie Chaplin, Frank, in the early days, was too tragic for a sensitive soul to appreciate. It was all a bit spiteful – you were always laughing directly at him.

But when they reinvented him for the second series of *Some Mothers Do ' Ave ' Em*, Frank Spencer became one of the funniest people ever to grace prime time TV, still a loser but less vulnerable and tragic – less worldly unwise even.

And so emerged Frank "I am he" Spencer. No longer reliant solely on the beret, an outrageous stunt to get us a wigglin' and a gigglin', Frank could look the world more squarely in the eye, take

With his new found eloquence, Frank greeted each new setback and challenge with a fascinating and infectious misplaced optimism.

less dramatic situations and have you rolling on the floor in hysterics without having to rely on roller-skating under an articulated lorry, church steeple helicopter rescues, or gigantic falling chimney-stacks chasing him down the road.

He had a sort of haphazard dignity now. He'd bounced back from an episode in the first series in which an exasperated psychiatrist confirmed that Frank was indeed a bona fide failure. It kind of took the weight off his shoulders somehow and he could now concentrate on life in the fast lane without getting depressed.

The feeling that he was as vulnerable and pathetic as a fragile mental patient was gone. Now he could confront people. If something didn't make sense, it was the other fella's fault.

Given the chance to deliver some hooky videos in the 'Demon King' episode in which he played a motorcycle messenger, he responded conspiratorially: "Say no more, Mr Hunt, a nod's as good as a limp." Bloody marvellous.

With his new-found eloquence, Frank

greeted each new setback and challenge with a fascinating and infectious misplaced optimism, usually punctuated by one of his mother's bizarre aphorisms.

A classic example occurred in the much-celebrated 'Columbo' episode. On his way home from the Chinese takeaway, Frank is relentlessly pursued by a mini-Collie. Frank pleads with the dog to desist.

"I am not your master," he says sternly as the dog sits down and stares at him. "Look, if you don't vacate the area I shall be forced to phone the police... I'm a married man!"

The dog stares sweetly and Frank is won over within seconds. Frank takes the dog home and presents him to his beleaguered wife Betty who, exasperated at this latest development in her perpetually half-mended, half-broken, half-baked world, vehemently argues against keeping the mutt. Frank, rabid with enthusiasm (he's figured it all out already) pleads: "But Betty, I think he could bring us a lot of luck. Just think, we found him on a Monday and you know what my mother always used to say on a Monday!?"

Betty: "What?"

Frank: "It's Monday."

Betty: "Oh."

Frank: "If you find a dog on a Monday, or anything starting with a 'D', like a deer or a duck, it might bring you luck... But then again it might not be..."

Frank Spencer's whole life is summed up in microscosm in the 'Demon King' episode when he ends up in court after being caught red-handed delivering the aforementioned mucky vids. Frank decides to defend himself after he discovers that his intended lawyers Whittle, Whittle & Crouch had either snuffed it ("legally diseased" Frank informs the Judge) or had conveniently gone AWOL.

One of the first to take the stand is the training officer from his RAF days who scathingly intimates that Frank was a few streaks of Danish shy of a bacon

> **'Ahh, sit down Frank, sit down Frank – that's been the story of my life. Frustration, frustration. For years all my passages have been blocked.'**

sandwich during an aptitude test. Frank is outraged and launches into an impassioned speech.

Frank: "Yesss... he made out like I was an idiot. 'Sit down Frank, stand up Frank. That's all he said to me. Put the wood in the hole, take the wood out of the hole'. Is that how you get your recruits? Is that how all the men turn blue? Did Douglas Bader have to put his wood in the hole? Did Group Captain Cheshire have to pull it out?"

Judge: "Mr Spencer sit down!"

Frank (hitting back with surprising venom): "Ahh, sit down Frank, sit down Frank – that's been the story of my life. Frustration, frustration. For years all my passages have been blocked."

Frank momentarily sits down before leaping up again in a scene as passionate and heartfelt as anything in *Twelve Angry Men*. This is a man who could take no more.

"I shall come back, I have more to say. I'm a rate payer, I have the right to say what I like. No wonder people are leaving the country and going hither and thither and willy nilly. Well if I had my way I'd... wither... my... hither... and (retreating sharply)... and anyway."

Judge: "Silence!"

Frank sits down and begins to look slightly worried. Rhetoric aside, he knows he could get three years in the chokey for this caper.

Frank: "I've still got a bit more to come."

Judge: "SILENCE!"

Frank (defiantly): "But I'm reachin' where I've always wanted to get to."

Judge (banging hammer down with wig askew): "SILENCE."

Frank: "...and there I rest the case for the defence."

After several outbursts, the Judge rules that Frank is clearly incapable of rational thinking and gives an apologetic, if totally understandable, 'diminished responsibility' verdict.

Frank is exalted, he's sure that it was his water-tight defence that got him off.

"Ahhh," he coos triumphantly to the bemused courtroom "as I leave this court with my blemishes unblemished desullied and all my morals intact, I thank you from the bottom of my heart. Or, as the immortal bard once wrote when he quilled The Shylock of the Anna... 'the quality of mercy is not strained, but it tinkles like a winkle... from above.'"

Frank raises his head to confront a deserted courtroom. "Ahhh," he says to Betty, "they've all gone... aaaahhh Betty, British justice must be done and not just done but seen and now I've seen it done to me, I know how done I've been."

Never surrender. Frank Spencer – truly a Great Living Englishman.

Tim Southwell

Harold Steptoe

January 1996

SOME MONTHS AGO, I dropped a line to some hack from one of the posher Sunday papers. "Dear Sir," the missive began, "With all due respect, you are a jumping jackass of the first order. May the fleas of a thousand and one camels infest the hair on your balls for all eternity." The inkslinger in question had got my dander

up good and proper by writing a column about *Steptoe & Son* in which he claimed that the show's enduring popularity was entirely due to the comic genius of Wilfred Brambell. This is a point of view which has become increasingly more fashionable in recent years – as though Harry H Corbett's contribution to the classic sitcom amounted to little more than a solid supporting role. However, if the recent TV repeats have taught us

anything, they have served as a reminder to all right-thinking people that Corbett's 'Arold Steptoe was at least half the reason for the show's direct appeal to the funny-bone. And that, more often than not, he stole the show from under Brambell's hooked nose.

Corbett was playing Macbeth at Bristol's Old Vic when, in 1961, writers Alan Simpson and Ray Galton invited him to take the role of the younger Steptoe. "I knew I had to do it the minute I finished reading the script," he said later. "It was full of pathos and huge belly-laughs. The perfect recipe for good comedy. But I had no idea it would be so successful. I thought 'I'll do a series of this and then get back to the theatre.' As it turned out 'Arold Steptoe took over my life."

A measure of the show's early success can be gauged by the fact that Harold Wilson, fearing that it would keep Labour voters away from the polling stations, begged the BBC to take it off air on the night of the 1964 elections. The BBC duly obliged and Wilson later claimed it won him the extra 13 seats in parliament. Between 1962 and 1974, it dominated the TV ratings, regularly pulling in up to 28 million viewers. Even so, Corbett was unconvinced that it would endure. "Sure," he'd say, "it makes people laugh like drains. But, let's be honest, it will be forgotten about in 20 years time. That's the nature of television. Unfortunately."

How wrong he was. More than 20 years on, enthusiasm for *Steptoe & Son* seems to grow with each season of repeats. And it becomes glaringly obvious, to all but the certified mad, that Corbett's masterly portrayal of the frustrated bachelor son was largely responsible for elevating it to those humdinging heights. In 'Arold Steptoe, Galton and Simpson created sitcom's most loveable chump; a character that Charlie Dickens would have given his left kidney for. But it was left to Corbett to bring him to life. Indeed, Corbett himself was instrumental in creating the 'Arold Steptoe look: rakish cap, dirty scarf, crusty boots and flapping overcoat. Like everything else about the character it was exactly right; as right as ninepence.

Each episode would find our 'Arold conspiring to escape the clutches of his snivelling, miserly old man, struggling to better himself in the face of Albert's wily ruses. And every episode without fail was sodding priceless. None more so than 'Wallah-Wallah Catsmeat' from 1963, in which the laughs start rolling from the off with old man Steptoe dropping fag ash all over 'Arold's cornflakes. And those laughs never let up until the curtain falls to the evocative clip-clop melody of that

wonderful theme tune. 'Arold, it soon transpires, has been offered 25 quid by the Cat Meat Man to part with the old man's beloved horse, Hercules. "A great horse like that," the young Steptoe enthuses, "he'd fill a few thousand tins." And so the plot unravels as ever with 'Arold forced to eat his words as the unfortunate nag falls sick. Along the way, the laughter comes in the usual tidal waves. But, as ever, an element of pathos is forever loitering in the wings ready to pounce. And so it proves when 'Arold, provoked beyond endurance by the old

> **'People often assume that I'm just like 'Arold,' Corbett would say, 'and it really pisses me off. How would you like to be mistaken for an emotionally retarded rag-and-bone man?'**

man's belly-aching, suggests a suicide pact. "Let's all go together," he says to Albert. "You, me and the horse. One wallop with the steam iron – you won't feel a thing. Nothing wrong with being dead... It's the living bit that frightens me."

It was lines like that, worthy of Sam Beckett himself, that gave *Steptoe & Son* a dramatic depth that most other British sitcoms could only daydream about. But that wasn't

all. In Albert and 'Arold *Steptoe* had characters finely drawn in a way that only *Fawlty Towers* and *Rising Damp* ever equalled. And the Steptoes' never-to-be-resolved relationship led them into situations that provided shit-stopping laughs every time.

With 'Arold Steptoe, Harry H Corbett created a sitcom great that is right up there with Basil Fawlty and Rigsby at the top of the effing Xmas tree. Like Cleese and Rossiter, Corbett himself was always at pains to distance himself from his character. "People often assume that I'm just like 'Arold," he'd say, "and it really pisses me off. How would you like to be mistaken for an emotionally retarded rag-and-bone man?" Equally, Corbett never made a secret of the regret he felt that the success of Steptoe derailed his career as a serious stage actor. When the show finally cashed in its chips in 1974, Corbett returned to the stage and won his fair share of acclaim. But it was as 'Arold Steptoe that he was destined to be remembered. He cashed in his own chips in 1982, with Wilfred Brambell following suit shortly after. You can imagine them now, up there somewhere in the abode of the blessed... Albert, screwing up that misshapen testicle of a face and hollering "Aaaaaar-old!!!", 'Arold himself wiping his nose on his scarf and muttering, "You durrr-ty old man!" Back of the net, mate. Every bleeding time.
Jon Wilde

Sweep

June 1997

THE GALLAGHER BROTHERS, constantly bickering with each other, smashing things up – they're rank amateurs. At the outset of punk in the mid '70s, anarchy was the watchword of the day. 'Destroy', said Johnny Rotten's T shirt. "IIIIIIII, wanna beeeeeeeeyah... anarchy," he sang. He was old hat too. Anarchy was already well known to the kids, and a generation before them too, courtesy of a bald man with his hands stuck up the greatest double act since Caesar and Mark Antony: Sooty and Sweep.

Why a yellow bear, his panda girlfriend and a dog should be friends is anyone's guess, but Sooty lorded it over the trio like the smug git he was, with his useless magic wand. A strange hierarchy existed where Sooty was the undisputed leader in the public's eye, yet was almost mute and could only communicate by going in close on Harry Corbett's ear, later replaced by son Matthew's ear. Sue, the panda bird,

she could speak perfect English and seemed to be up for it more than any other panda in known history. Then, squeaking hysterically, flapping his ears as he went manic and destroyed everything around him like a

Squeaking hysterically, flapping his ears as he went manic and destroyed everything around him like a demented boom microphone, was Sweep.

demented boom microphone, was Sweep. Always the underdog, the kid desperately vying for the attention that went to the undeserving piece of yellow matting who was constantly putting him down, Sweep was driven to the dark side of madness by the golden child on the other hand. Sooty had magic on his side, but his tricks were always crap, the results transient and hollow, and when they didn't work he flew into a rage, usually with a water pistol. But for all that, Sooty was wholesome and knew it, milking his kiddy popularity for all he could with his cuteness and speech blockage. Secretive, he spoke only to the master – cavorting with the establishment – and left Sweep out of it, on the edges. They were Lennon and McCartney, both controlled and driven by the same higher force leaving Sue as some sort of furry Yoko with an unseen hand up her back passage. Even now, take a look at Yoko Ono in her stupid big sunglasses, black patches on a pale face, and see if you can tell the difference. Yoko, Japanese; pandas, Chinese – these are the facts.

Sweep's lot was a constant struggle against his nemesis and, by twist of fate, best friend. His was the anarchic, creative genius that would burst forth in actions like dipping his head in a bowl of flour, starting a water fight or just squeaking a lot and repeatedly banging his head on a table. Works of genius every time, leaving the safe stuff to the so-called star of the show. Sooty had carefully considered craft, but Sweep was pure instinctual art.

Surviving the sad death of Harry Corbett, Sweep lost none of his genius

when given a new lease of life by the new generation, Matthew. Just as Sooty never lost his bland, play safe attitude and his pathetic attempts at copying his friend, whom he knew to be much more talented. Success was not enough, and still in the dark hours, it eats away at Sooty's soul to know he is more popular, yes, but touched by the gods

Never has a puppet dog with a hand up his arse been so important and never has the man with the hand up the arse been arrested.

of comedy genius like Sweep is, no.

While they enjoy a worldwide resurgence in popularity today, Sooty still wields his wholesome wand while Sweep continues to sneer, well, as close to

sneering as you can get when your mouth's a line of stitched wool and the only sound you can make is "eep".

Never has a puppet dog with a hand up his arse been so important and never has the man with the hand up the arse been arrested.

Sweep, your genius and devastating madness stand for all time, laughing at the wannabes and rock stars who can't hold a candle to you. Presumably in case they set you on fire.
Derek Harbinson

Trigger

July 1996

THE HISTORY OF COMEDY was written on the fat backs of complete morons like Trigger, the road sweeper div from *Only Fools And Horses*, a modern day fusion of Stan Laurel, a village idiot, and fungus. And all the best comedy the world has ever seen has been the comedy that reminds you you're human and that you're still basically the bumbling idiot your PE teacher said you were.

For the most part, you feel sorry for Trigger, that he's an idiot and a fool, the classic 'doesn't know his arse from his elbow' case. But this is just a red herring since at the end of the day, you'll end up laughing because he'll deliver one of the greatest pay-offs you've heard of in years. He won't seem so helpless when he's made Del look like an idiot in front of Boycie, by letting it slip that Del's been giving Marlene one on the quiet for the last 20 years.

We first discovered Trigger when he walked in the bar of the Nag's Head in Peckham to meet his mate Del Boy back in the mid-80s. Since then he's become one of the most endearing characters in British life – everyone knows Trigger.

A dimwitted road sweeper in a brown suit, who had no social graces and yet, at the same time, knew enough to bury every man in the pub.

Trigger was an ambling mess. About six foot three, lanky, with browny black hair, he had an expression like the skin on a bowl of Ready Brek. He was a loafer,

stupidity personified and presented in a neat package with a label reading 'dunce'. We all knew him, Christ, most of the time we felt like him when he walked up to Del and his brother Rodney.

Trigger to Rodney: "Hello Dave."

Del Boy to Trigger: "You know my brother, don't you Trigger?"

Trigger: "Course. Awright Dave."

Trigger goes to the bar.

Rodney to Del: "Why is he called Trigger, is it cos he carries a gun?"

Del: "No, it's because he looks like a horse."

Fantastic. And that was it. His path through the next few programmes was set. Trigger was to be the fool, the man who embarrassed those around him, who set the other up and who took the prat-falls.

A dimwitted road sweeper in a brown suit, who had no social graces and yet, at

Rodney to Del: 'Why is he called Trigger, is it cos he carries a gun?' Del: 'No, it's because he looks like a horse.'

the same time, knew enough to bury every man in the pub.

Perhaps one of the best instances of Trigger's naïve brilliance was when Del tried to stitch up Rodney. Both were competing for Trigger's niece and she was having none of it. Del left Rodney under a sun lamp the night before his date, leaving his little brother looking like a panda in Magaluf zoo. Rodney returned the favour by letting Del hang-glide off a cliff, leaving him in the air for hours

before he crashed into a pylon and fell through some bloke's sunroof. Del turned up back at the flat after coming out of hospital in a wheelchair. He couldn't move and told Rodney he was disabled and stuck in a wheelchair for life. Rodney couldn't believe it. He turned to Trigger and asked how they got back to the flat.

"Oh, we come here in a Green Line bus," said Trigger, blowing Del's whole game up the wall. There was no way the hospital was going to let a cripple out on public transport.

This was Trigger's problem, life just left him behind, he couldn't get a grip, he was never up to speed. A greatest living Englishman because his heart was as big as the world, his mind as small as a peanut. That's what made this country great, y'know?

Tim Southwell

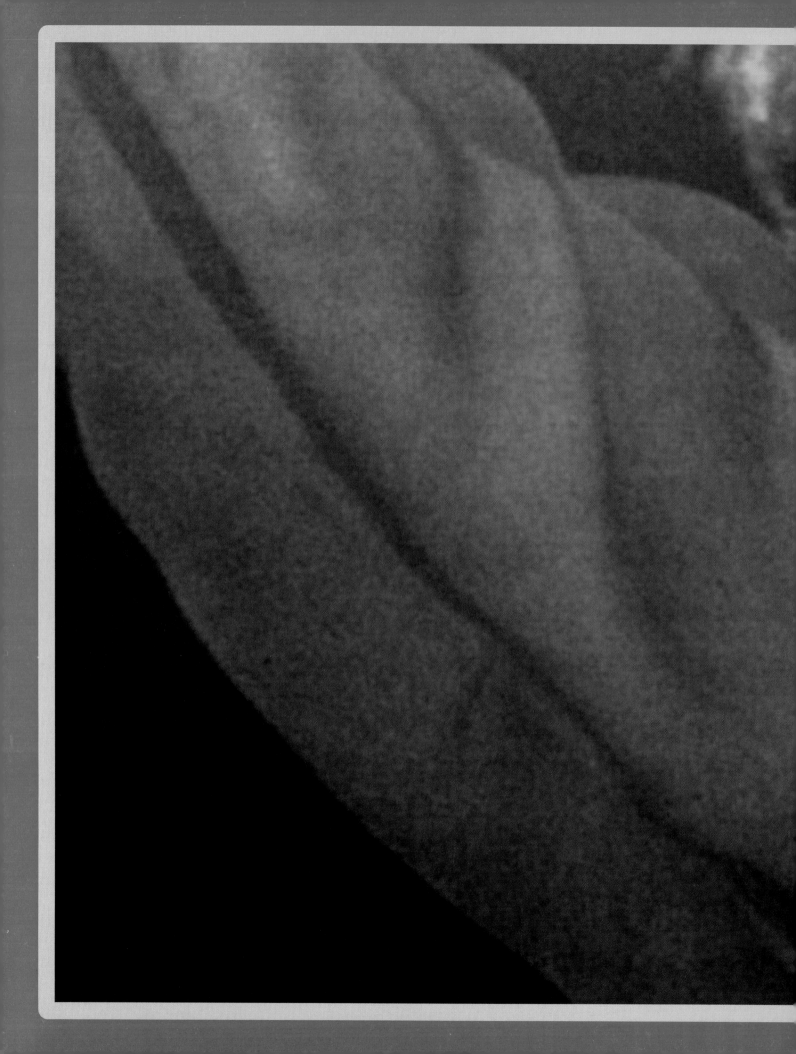

Rock Stars

Ted Chippington

February 1996

WHO? Most of you are going to ask as you check out this month's Greatest Living Englishman. Well let me tell you, we've had cod philosophers, barmen, voice-over merchants, women, dead South African actors and even a talking fox, but I can assure you this largely forgotten mid-'80s cult comedy star, Ted Chippington, deserves to be right in there amidst them all.

It's 1985 at the Fforde Grene pub in Harehills, Leeds, the venue is a regular haunt of no longer fashionable bands, folk artists, and reggae outfits. Rastas and bikers hang around the pool room wondering where the chalk went, ex-rock stars in the next room wonder where the fans went. For hippy combo Here & Now this wasn't too much of a problem, the spotlight of cool credibility had never really scorched their skins but they still maintained a loyal following.

I was there to see some mates in the support act, and expected nothing more than that. I certainly didn't expect to stumble across the funniest performer in Britain. But on he came, a curious sight. Receding up front with long straggly hair down to his collar. And what a collar, grotesquely flowered, like his shirt which was worn under the striped woollen tank top. The whole uncomfortable image was completed by black Oxford bags and stack heels. Something was wrong. People didn't dress like this in the mid '80s.

As Ted moved slowly into his routine it became apparent that he had either suffered some sort of blackout that had lasted about 12 years, or was simply operating on a totally different plane to anyone else. People talk about the creative isolation of Lenny Bruce, but when it comes to a manifesto of solitude,

Lenny was working Wembley Arena compared to Ted.

Most of Chippington's 'jokes' lasted about 35 seconds and were delivered with all the passion of a moribund talking clock. In between the two-liners he would respond to scant applause and frequent heckles with such humble comments as "Cheers Chief" and "Can't be bad". Still, for every 50 people in the room there was one person who was perfectly in tune with the bizarre simplicity of the jokes. Hysterical cackles in the darkness can do a lot for mood enhancement.

As the short set rambled on it became apparent that Ted's jokes nearly all started "Walking down the road the other day..."

He skips clumsily through those avenues of skillful incompetence first dug by the late, great Tommy Cooper.

For instance, "Walking down the road the other day this long-haired chap came up to me. He said 'do you want some grass?' I said 'No thanks, pal, I've got crazy paving.'" Or, "Walking down the road the other day this drug addict came up to me and said 'I'm addicted.' I said, 'I'm sure you are mate.'" The audience would clap, Ted would answer, "Cheers", pause for a sip of his pint, point out it was nice to have a sip of a pint during a performance and move on to another deadpan delivery in a flat Brummie accent.

The pinnacle of the evening came with the classic "Walking down the road the other day this bloke came up to me and said 'How far is it to the railway station?'" Ted replied in a gruff voice, "'One mile' 'One mile?' 'Aye [gruff again]. Roughly speaking.'"

Such was the audience response it was clear that Ted Chippington was going places, albeit very slowly in the back of an articulated lorry. Using rock concerts as the only available forum to perform – a route pursued by both Vic Reeves and Mark Lamarr – Ted gradually became the sought-after support act for left-field bands. Mark E Smith of The Fall, who had himself worn garish fashions to annoy punks and critics alike, championed Chippington and his name began to crop up regularly alongside such rare acts as The Nightingales and 5 Go Down to the Sea.

At the time the *New Musical Express* commented: "Ted Chippington is a genius. Never once in his seven year long career has he needed to change a single line of his six-joke repertoire... He skips clumsily through those avenues of skillful incompetence first dug by the late, great Tommy Cooper."

The concert that propelled Ted into the babbling brook that was the mainstream of the early indie scene was the legendary *Royal Iris* boat trip

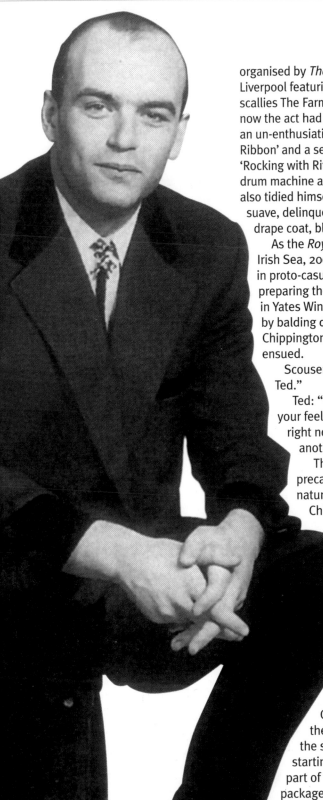

organised by *The End* magazine of Liverpool featuring John Peel, local scallies The Farm and Ted Chippington. By now the act had been expanded to include an un-enthusiatic version of 'Tie A Yellow Ribbon' and a self-penned number 'Rocking with Rita' set to a rudimentary drum machine and backing track. Ted had also tidied himself up, appearing as a suave, delinquent rockabilly with sombre drape coat, black jeans and boppers.

As the *Royal Iris* sailed out into the Irish Sea, 200 fashion-crazy scousers in proto-casual gear who'd been preparing themselves for three hours in Yates Wine Lodge were confronted by balding deadpan comedian Ted Chippington. A true battle of wits ensued.

Scousers: "Fuck off Ted, fuck off Ted."

Ted: "Cheers chiefs, appreciate your feelings but can't fuck off right now. I might get wet. Here's another one."

The atmosphere balanced precariously between good-natured and violent but Chippington won the crowd over. John Peel was so impressed with the performance that when the same line-up was booked for the following year's charity cruise he broadcast the event on his Radio One show.

From there Chippington moved out of the hard shoulder and into the slow lane. Things were starting to happen. Signed as part of a subsidiary label package to a major company – punky Bananarama types Fuzzbox being the bait – it wasn't long before Ted found himself on *Pebble Mill*, *Whistle Test* and a national tour promoting The Vindaloo Records Summer package single, and even encountering a brief skirmish with the arse-end of the Top Twenty.

His set was expanded to include more songs and now featured almost 12 jokes, still based around the original "Walking down the road the other day..." formula. For instance: "Walking down the road the other day, a bloke pulled up, rolled down his window and said, 'I'm in a dilemma.' Nice motors, dilemmas."

Yet as Chippington prospered on his new-found cult status amongst beer monsters and students who flocked to his now 500-strong gigs to chant out punch lines and catchphrases, cynical critics who failed to find anything funny about a balding man delivering comedy at morgue pace were increasingly voluminous in wondering "Is that it?"

The latter began to out-shout the former and Chippington became marked by the media as a passing freak, a flavour of the minute. Despite recording an album, the moment indeed passed and

A balding man delivering comedy at morgue pace... politically incorrect for his day but hilarious all the same.

Ted disappeared quietly. The last time I saw him perform he had introduced one new slightly different joke. Politically incorrect for the day but hilarious all the same: "My wife came in the other day and found me doing the washing up. She said 'You've got those gloves on the wrong hands.' I said 'I know, they should be on yours.'" He was again ahead of his time.

A great fan of trucking music, by the end of the '80s Chippington had followed his dream and moved to Atlantic Beach, California, taking his chip pan – he was a great maker of chips – his Fall records and his quietly inspired humour with him. And there, for the moment, rested the dormant talent of a truly individual comedian. Ted Chippington was an inspired performer and good company. You can't say fairer than that. Top entertainment.
James Brown

Ian Dury

July 2000

HE WAS NOT YOUR average pop star, Ian Dury. With his limp and his stick, his grizzled, cratered features (that, even on a good day, resembled a long-disused quarry) and a singing voice that was, quite frankly, as rough as a raven's crotch. About as far from the average pop star as you can get. Then again, there was nothing average about Ian Dury. One of the last of the genuine geezers, with a bastard of a talent to boot.

That mighty talent was snuffed out a couple of months back when the Big C finally got the better of the loveable old

There was nothing average about Ian Dury: one of the last of the genuine geezers, with a bastard of a talent to boot.

cove. But he leaves behind a body of work ('Hit Me With Your Rhythm Stick', 'Reasons To Be Cheerful (Pt 3)' etc) that will still be raising one hell of a laugh when most of his contemporaries have slipped through the cracks of history. Dury knew it all along. "I'm cocky dicky about my words," he said. "And I've always thought that I didn't have any competition. I'm the best in the world by 100 miles."

Having tried his hand at painting and teaching, he started doing music as a joke in the early '70s. A lengthy stretch on the pub rock scene yielded little in the way of acclaim. Until, that is, he formed the Blockheads just as punk arrived. "Pub rock with a bit of jazz and funk malarkey on top" was how Dury described their sound. A good few whoops and hollers from your standard punk thrash. Elton John famously but inaccurately described Dury as the Roy Hudd of rock 'n' roll, but he was more like punk's Noel Coward – possessed of a crafty wit, a precious gift for cock-eyed observation and a way with Cockney rhyming couplets second to none, all of which he brought to bear on his cheeky three-minute musical vignettes that both celebrated and mocked the nature of England and Englishness.

The characters that inhabited his best songs were worthy of Peter Cook and Alan Bennett combined. Plaistow Patricia, Clever Trevor and the ever-randy Billericay Dickie. Best of all, perhaps, was one of the crew of mad suburbanites found in his 1979 song 'This Is What We Find': "Harold Hill... Of do-it-yourself dexterity and double-glazing skill/Who came home to find another gentleman's kippers in the grill/So he sanded off his winkle with a Black & Decker drill." If Larkin or

'There ain't half been some clever bastards,' he once wrote. And Dury was indeed one of them.

Betjeman wrote a better line, then there's three buttocks to every bum.

By his own admission, Dury's songwriting muse began to desert him in the early '80s. With the Blockheads on hold, he turned instead to TV and theatre, with mixed results. He was always in demand though. Even Andrew Lloyd Webber begged his services in adapting the lyrics for the musical Cats. "I said no, straight off," said Dury. "Andrew Lloyd Webber's a cunt, isn't he?" Yes.

Occasionally, when the fancy took him, Dury would regroup the band and knock off albums that never quite recaptured

the robust spirit of his late "on stage" work – until 1998's near impeccable *Mr Love Pants*, by which time he had been diagnosed with cancer. True to form, he fought out the illness with customary grace and chirpy humour. "I've had a good run," he told one reporter. "Mustn't grumble. No point feeling sorry for myself. 'Sorry for myself' is for wankers, innit?"

No surprise, then, that when he did finally snuff it, he was chuckling away to the very last, finding a reason to be cheerful even at death's door. "There ain't half been some clever bastards," he once wrote. And Dury was indeed one of them. Clever bastard. Diamond geezer. Champion blockhead.
Jon Wilde

Tony Hadley

July 1998

"'WHEN you're just one door of a small house in a very big council estate, then looking different from everyone else becomes a very crucial aspect of your life." – Tony Hadley, 1982.

Spandau Ballet were about being different. Posing on stage like a bunch of second-hand-car-dealing matadors, this much was obvious. What none of the newspapers could work out was what they actually stood for.

After the bloody demise of the Pistols and punk, the press just wasn't ready for a well-behaved underground movement. Spandau were about suburban escapism. Whereas punk involved sliding around in pools of gob and toppling the fascist junta, Spandau's political agenda stopped just short of doing it all night with sexy birds. From one rare appearance to the next they could look like either Cossack binmen or millionaire cocktail waiters. They were clean and polite and your mum loved them. They were smoother than lager, yet as uniquely British as the dubbin on your football boots. Alongside Visage and Duran Duran they were the New Romantics, and Tony Hadley was the king. They didn't want to tear up the world so much as put on a couple of slow tunes and squeeze its bum till it giggled.

Spandau Ballet was actually born on 17 November, 1979. Hadley, Gary and Martin Kemp, Steve Norman and John Keeble took their name from a bit of graffiti on a prison wall in Berlin. Their first gig took place in a rented studio where 50 invited 'Blitz kid' guests were blown away by the band's blend of new soul and old-style crooning.

Lead singer Hadley was clearly the successor to a line of romantic English

On being asked by a journalist why he was playing in a gay club, Hadley retorted: 'Not on our night it won't be.'

frontmen stretching back to Bowie and Bolan. At just 19 years of age, wearing "slightly Puerto Rican" balloon trousers with cross-over crotch and a hand-embroidered shirt, he tried to explain the essence of his band: "We're not like the punks and mods, we don't believe in all wearing the same thing. Everyone has their own theme, whatever they fancy – the show starts the minute the first fan walks through the door."

Hadley was as close as you could get to James Bond if you worked in Gateway's. He had single-handedly made it acceptable for blokes who would normally be out robbing old people to saunter around the local Wimpy dressed like Lionel Blair. It was clear his music had become the accompaniment to a new, swellegant way of living.

Heart-throb Tony was quite unashamedly narcissistic: "What everyone gets wrong about this whole thing is that they stand back and say, 'We can't afford to do that!' That is absolute

crap. We were on the dole for like six months and we still had style!"

In 1980, and now sporting dark gaucho's trousers (tucked into spats and boots), with billowing fawn blousons and bright sashes, they signed with Chrysalis Records for a cool £85,000. The first album, 1981's *Journey To Glory*, was a classic piece of white disco funk. Dressed up like extras off *The Flashing Blade*, they played the Underground club in New York. Calvin Klein, De Niro and Dusty from *Dallas* were all in the audience. Hadley came back to England a star.

The ex-*My Guy* model had always been one for the ladies. On being asked by a journalist why he was playing in a gay club, he retorted: "Not on our night it won't be," adding that he hoped a lot of "birds" would come along to the gig. They did. The papers called it Balletomania. When their second album, *Diamond,* came out – featuring the singles 'True' and 'Gold' – Spandau suddenly had Number Ones in 22 countries. Their disco anthems had become the soundtrack to Thatcher's yuppie boom. In 1983 Tony married his secretary girlfriend Leonie and the band stormed Europe. After their gear was nicked in Portugal they had to improvise, and manufactured new stage costumes by ripping up hotel bed sheets. They'd routinely turn up in the papers hanging around Bahaman pools wearing thongs like some rent-boy pressure group. In

1984, Tony refused to play any large venues in LA on the grounds they didn't have enough style. When they finally ended up playing the Wilshire Theater, several girls had to be removed after

Whereas punk involved sliding around in pools of gob and toppling the fascist junta, Spandau's political agenda stopped just short of doing it all night with sexy birds.

having hysterical fits. "I don't know why I have this effect," said Tony. "My wife just laughs it off." He was chronically normal.

"I'm not into being pulled by women. If I ever wanted to pull I'd do it myself. It's really vulgar of them. You might as well go to a brothel. You don't have a clue who they are – they might have dirty underwear, dandruff and greasy hair. I just take the mickey out of them when they hand me the keys to their rooms."

After 18 months of marriage and the birth of his first child, he seemed to have his life worked out: "When I come back blotto, falling about hitting walls and completely unable to speak, Leonie never

complains. She just helps me into bed, pulls my clothes off and tucks me in... When you get married you have to decide to stay faithful. Having a little bit on the side just doesn't work. If you're into sheer animal lust then you shouldn't get married. The night I first met Leonie I said, 'That's it, I'm going out with you, you're my bird.' The best thing about her is that she always wakes me up with a cup of tea, which is my idea of heaven."

In 1986 Spandau Ballet reached the peak of their success with their *Through The Barricades* album. They went on their longest tour ever, which culminated in Tony vandalising a posh Italian hotel in a £15,000 wrecking spree. He also destroyed £3,000 worth of antiques and wrote off six cars by taking their handbrakes off and pushing them down a hill.

"I don't know what came over me, I've never done anything like this before. I jumped on top of the cars and ran up and down the bonnets and roofs causing even more damage."

An aide claimed he was suffering from 'road fever' but a more realistic cause might have been that the popularity of the band was on the wane. The single 'Raw', taken from the album *Heart Like A Sky* was a modest hit. And with the Kemps rumoured to be starring in an upcoming film about the Krays, Spandau's days were numbered. Though the band never split, Tony went solo, released an eponymous album that's been massive in Europe, and this year even sang the national anthem at the FA Cup final. It was a fine thing indeed to see Tony standing on the hallowed turf of Wembley banging out 'Abide With Me' in true Spandau style. It's just a shame he didn't go the extra yard and do it dressed up like a berk.

Phil Robinson

Steve Jones

October 1996

In the reformed Pistols' first interview, Jonesy found a feature on streakers in a magazine. 'Look at them big tits!' he enthused.

AT LAST THE TRUE HERO of the Sex Pistols can be revealed: a man who has devoted 20 years to shagging and heroic underachievement – stand up, Steve 'Fatty' Jones. Never mind Johnny Rotten's vitriol against the Queen's fascist regime or Sid Vicious and his dum-dum by nihilism. Forget 'Anarchy in the UK'. It was always clear what Steve Jones stood for – shagging and plenty of it.

"Socially, I've been shagging as many birds as possible," he announced in a 1978 interview. He listed his interest as "Birds, any birds." There was a glorious moment when the conversation turned to Pauline, the deranged woman whom the Pistols wrote 'Bodies' about. Now on any scale, pulling a bird who carries an aborted foetus in her bag is hardly a result. Unless you were Steve Jones that is. "Met her, I've shagged her an' all, round the back of the Marquee it was!" he proudly declared.

Jonesy's record was shagging five birds in one evening. His first two conquests were at the Nashville Club: "Not at the same time mind you but I took them out to the car in this alley I know. Then I went down to the Speakeasy and got another two, right? The same treatment, they didn't mind. Then I went down to the Embassy Club, a right posh place in Bond Street. I pulled one there. I didn't bother taking her to the car cos she was too nice. So I took her home." What a true romantic.

Steve seemed to suffer from an excess of testosterone. After all, this was a man who masturbated over a hot dog and then gave it to the despised Glen Matlock. His Pistols career featured other heroic moments: wearing that knotted handkerchief on his head for the 'Pretty Vacant' video; calling Bill Grundy a "filthy fucker" and a "fucking rotter"; and the moment at the Randy's Rodeo 'Battle of the Alamo' gig in the States when, confronted by Texas rednecks throwing cans and bottles, Jonesy simply headed the offending missiles away like a burly centre half.

When the Pistols split, Jones and drummer Paul Cook confessed everything to the music press: "We're just a couple of working class tossers. We was only in for the birds, the booze and the piss-ups." And no one made a better working class tosser than Steve Jones.

He had spent much of his youth banged up in approved schools for nicking cars. His only job was three weeks as a window cleaner: "You used to get birds asking you in for a cup of tea like and you end up in bed with them." Most of the Pistols' equipment was stolen, claimed the light-fingered guitarist. "Steve had a lot of street suss, but not being able to read or write did make things a little difficult," explained Rotten.

But by the simple means of "giving it some bollocks", Steve Jones, illiterate tea leaf, emerged as the greatest power-chord merchant in pop history. After the

Pistols he should have become a guitar legend. Instead he turned underachievement into an art form.

Post-Rotten there was the cash-in single 'No One is Innocent', filmed on a Brazilian beach with Ronnie Biggs. It was a true meeting of minds – Jones and Biggs instantly bonded with their tales of burglary and birds. "Steve Jones, Paul Cook and Ronnie Biggs, we're the next best thing," announced Jones. They weren't.

The rather good 'Silly Thing' followed, along with Jonesy's heartfelt vocal contribution to 'Friggin in the Riggin', a song about shagging that began with 'It was on the good ship Venus...'. But Sid died and the remaining Pistols folded. Cook and Jones teamed up with a hippy called Andy and recorded an album with The Professionals. Good name. Shame the album bombed.

Jones then moved to LA where he proceeded to make Billy Idol look like a chaste workaholic. The perpetual encore guitarist, Jones never actually formed a successful band in 13 years. There were brushes with drug and alcohol addictions, an ignored solo album, some guitar work on Iggy Pop's *Blah, Blah Blah* album... and that's it. His latest dodgy outfit is The Neurotic Outsiders with John Taylor and Duff McKagan of Guns 'n' Roses.

Then after 18 years of heroic loafing came the news of the Pistols reforming. Had failure changed Steve Jones? In the reformed Pistols' first interview, Jonesy found a feature on streakers in a magazine. "Look at them big tits!" he enthused.

'Steve had a lot of street suss, but not being able to read or write did make things a little difficult,' explained Rotten.

The Finsbury Park gig gloriously reaffirmed his commitment to shagging and rock 'n' roll indulgence. There was Jonesy, fat and 40, unwisely squeezed into strides and arms around Stuart Pearce and Gareth Southgate. His one comment to the audience of ageing punks was, "Who wants a shag?" Could the boy still give it some bollocks on guitar? Of course he could. Creation Records boss Alan McGee took out a full page advert to announce that the Pistols were better than his Oasis charges.

And amid all the punk retrospective nonsense, it took Jonesy to never mind the bollocks. Standing by his LA swimming pool, fag in hand and stripped to the waist to expose his tattoos, the flabby old fornicator announced on BBC2's *Dancing In The Street*: "I was brought up in Shepherd's Bush, I hardly went to school. I didn't know who the Prime Minister was. I just wanted to play and get hold of some birds."

Steve Jones, we salute you: the working class tosser, the greatest living English shagger.
Pete May

Morrissey

February 1998

MORRISSEY turned me gay. Oh come on, admit it, he turned you gay too. In fact, Morrissey single-handedly turned the entire *nation* gay. Not gay in the boys-who-like-boys-who like-moustaches sense, *obviously*. We wouldn't want to suggest that Morrissey is *actually* a lifter of other gentlemen's floral print shirts. Oh no. But gay in the note-to-get-off-games, no-interest-in-football, can't-hold-their-ale sense. Having no friends, sitting in graveyards feeling sad, writing terrible self-indulgent poetry that will be discovered after you're dead, and then they'll all be sorry and painting your bedroom walls black as a mirror of your soul. You remember, it was called the '80s.

Y'see, you have to remember just how much of a rebel-with-a-Russ-Abbot-quiff Morrissey really was. At the time The Smiths flounced into pop's back pantry around 1984, everyone was being disgustingly upbeat. George 'I love men' Michael was dancing on *Top Of The Pops* in a T-shirt emblazoned with the slogan 'Choose Life', Boy 'I love Jesus' George was dancing like a paper doily fairy and singing "war is stupid" and Holly 'Condoms? Pah!' Johnson was mooing about 'The Power of Love'. Even being blind was great, what with Lionel Richie groping the disabled and Stevie Wonder indulging in public phone sex. Unemployed? On strike? Been viciously bayoneted to death by Grant Mitchell in the South Atlantic? Ahh, Frankie Says 'RELAX'.

Then along came a skinny geek in National Health glasses, a string of pearls and a broken hearing aid. Singing about frankly dodgy sexual practices in a voice like a man badly in need of a decent decongestant. Good God. Suddenly here were songs which weren't boy-meets-girl-and-they-fall-in-love, they were more boy-

Morrissey single-handedly turned the entire nation gay.

meets-indeterminate-other-possibly-a-family-member-or-moors-murderer-and-loses-innocence-via-sordid-and-very-uncomfortable-sex. The very second the Mozzter whacked us around our wedge-heads with his gladioli we were instantly given an excuse to be proper teenagers: sullen, self-pitying and, above all, bloody miserable. Now, being pale, eating Linda McCartney's Very Expensive Soya Products and buying all your clothes from the Spastics Shop became deeply cool. More importantly, it became the only way to get off with girls. It was brilliant: The Sensitive Gambit.

But the fact that Morrissey existed at all seemed utterly outrageous. This was cultural terrorism in a world where rock stars were expected to:
a) Live in Transits, drink cider and shag groupies;
b) Live in a mansion, drink vintage brandy and shag film stars;

c) Die in an Australian hotel room, stuffed full of prescription drugs, with an orange shoved up your bottom.

Yet here was Morrissey warbling impossibly frank lyrics like, "There's a club, if you'd like to go/You could meet somebody who really loves you/So you go, and you stand on your own/And you leave on your own/And you go home, and you cry/And you want to die." How much more gay could anything GET?

Moz's lyrics swung from the near profound: "It's so easy to laugh/So easy to hate/It takes guts to be gentle and kind", to the brilliantly mental: "A boy in the bush is worth two in the hand/I think I can help you get through your exams."

Snoop Doggy Dogg was shipped from the country in leg irons for much lesser mind crimes.

But, best of all, Mozzer took to the pop star lark with an aplomb not seen since Steve Wright and The Afternoon Boys attempted a *third* single ('The Gay Cavalieros' light-perm fans). Morrissey had the tabloids hanging on his every well turned word simply by having the bottle to call Princess Diana ugly, Madonna a prostitute, Maggie Thatcher a murderer (also recommending she be shot) and dismissing the Band Aid record – at the time, on a par with Jezzer Christ's loaves and fishes gig – with the words, "One can have a great concern for the people of Ethiopia but it's another thing to inflict daily torture on the people of England."

Even when Moz was turning in badly stained, dog-eared homework like '89's frankly rubbish *Ouija Board, Ouija Board,* the *Sun* were still running gleeful headlines like, "Churchmen Brand Morrissey Record The Devil's Work", while adding that a spokesman for Christian Response To the Occult warned, "It's possible Morrissey will be demonised by his own record".

Often, however, Morrissey's ego/gob combination overshadowed the incredible music The Smiths were making. From the jaunty flower-wanging

Listen to 'How Soon Is Now', a vast, shuddering wave of swirling guitar that sounds like a cow being pushed into a giant pencil sharpener.

of 'Hand in Glove', 'Ask', 'Bigmouth Strikes Again' (Chorus: "Oh/Oh/Big-mou-houth/Ho-ho-Haha! Bigmouth/La-da-d-dah!") to the fantastic atmospherics of 'There Is A Light', 'Please, Please, Please Let Me Get What I Want' and 'That Joke Isn't Funny Anymore', Morrissey and Marr virtually invented indie guitar music single-handedly. Listen to 'How Soon Is Now', a vast, shuddering wave of swirling guitar that sounds like a cow being pushed into a giant pencil sharpener. Then compare and contrast with Ned's Atomic Dustbin. I rest my case.

Sadly, when The Smiths split up in 1987, Morrissey, well, became shit. Like so many before him – Bowie, Lou Reed, Chesney Hawkes – Mozz refused to admit that it was all over and continued to send flowers, leave messages on the answer phone and lurk around in the street at night, staring up at lit windows. His endless fascination with working-class kitchen-sink misery which inspired classics like 'This Night Has Opened My Eyes' and 'Sheila Take A Bow' withered into a sort of crazed cab driver-mentality, churning out baldly provocative shite like 'Bengali in Platforms', 'National Front Disco' and 'Poofs Can't Swim'. A sad situation made all the worse by recruiting failed ginger rockabillies The Polecats as his backing band.

OK, so Morrissey has turned into a fat *Carry On* cliché queen who fills his ever-lengthening days breeding cats, reading Babs Cartland and watching re-runs of *Mind Your Language*. And in photos, his head appears to be expanding like a waterlogged potato. But there was a time when the sun truly did shine out of his behind. Expect him in panto at the Salford Winter Gardens, 2007. Gary Barlow as Buttons.
John Perry

Kevin Rowland

June 1996

YOU DON'T GET TO HEAR much about Kevin Rowland these days. Every so often, there'll be a gutter press report about how he's down on his luck, without a nail to hang his arse on, signing on the Nat King Cole and all that. Now and again, you might read about how he's teamed up again with Big Jimmy 'The Trombone' Paterson and knuckled down to writing new songs – which never seem to materialise. On the face of it, there's nothing unusual about this. After all, former pop stars down on their luck are a dime a dozen. But it shouldn't need pointing out Kevin Rowland was no garden variety pop star. Mention his name to anyone remotely touched by his mad genius in the '80s and it's a certainty they'll draw a deep breath, look you square in the eye and say "Kevin Rowland is a fucking hero and you'd better believe it."

To recap, Dexy's Midnight Runners blew into town at the arse-end of 1979 with bowel-loosening intensity – their phenomenal impact all the more surprising as, just months previously, Kev had been dismissed as just another New Wave also-ran. Having served his time in pseudo-punk deadbeats The Killjoys, and stiffed big-time, it seemed as if his chance had gone. Then he disappeared into rehearsals for six months with the eight piece Dexy's, fashioning an attitude and a sound inspired in equal measures by Scorsese's *Mean Streets* and Sam & Dave's 'Soul Sister Brown Sugar'. The result was something to shit a pineapple over. "Shut your fucking mouth 'til you know the truth," went their debut single 'Dance Stance' and, as a declaration of intent, it couldn't have been bettered. The next single, 'Geno', went in at Number One and from then on they were unstoppable.

But it wasn't just the music that made Dexy's so tin-parachute special. It was the whole kit and caboodle. They wore donkey jackets and woolly hats, sat in caffs, drank tea and felt intense. They were smash-and-grab artists; deep-thinking misfits; wild-hearted outsiders to a man. And Kev was the most wild-hearted of them all.

It wasn't just the music that made Dexy's so tin-parachute special: they wore donkey jackets and woolly hats, sat in caffs, drank tea and felt intense.

For three solid years, he ruled the pop roost – and was the most contrary bastard. One for the grand gesture, he hijacked the master tapes of the first Dexy's LP to renegotiate his contracts with EMI. During live shows, he was known to assault members of the audience if he thought they weren't giving his band their undivided attention. He punched out a music journalist in the middle of High Holborn because he had been interviewed by the fellow in question and felt the hack hadn't grasped 'the absolute intensity' of Dexy's message. Once, it was said, he gave chase through London with a piece of scaffolding after a bloke who had suggested that Kev's woolly hat made him look a dead ringer for Benny out of *Crossroads*.

That trigger-happy intensity found full expression on his records, where he came over like a man who'd stop at nothing in his hell-bent pursuit of intense thought and expression. "Big Jimmy!" he implored on the first album (*Searching For The Young Soul Rebels*) "for God's sake, burn it down!" And so it continued through the magnificent second album, *Too-Rye-Ay*, where Kev and his gang went all folky and asked us to punish our bodies until we believed in our souls. They'd traded in their donkey jackets for dungarees and still cut the mustard despite looking like refugees from an amateur production of *Oliver Twist*.

Then, at the peak of the band's success, Kev disappeared for three years. When he re-emerged in 1986, togged out in pinstripe suit and brogues, he was more at loggerheads with pop convention than ever. The third album, *Don' t Stand Me Down*, was a sprawling work of psychotic genius which included extended Pinteresque chats between Kev and sidekick Billy Adams and flipped-out song cycles railing against obscure targets like people who put creases in

At a party recently he insisted on speaking entirely in dialogue from Spike Lee's *Do The Right Thing*, which offered some hope he'd rediscovered his old maverick touch.

their Levis. The live shows were no less barmy, Billy coming onstage dressed as a copper and arresting Kev for "being a bit too intense". It was all totally squirrelly. The public were distinctly underwhelmed. In 1988, Kev dressed up as a Spanish matador to promote a country-flavoured solo album entitled *The Wanderer* – which offered fleeting reminders of the old razzle dazzle. But it sold like a dull thud and Kev was promptly given the old heave-ho by his record company.

In 1990, he hit the headlines after doing a runner from a West End bar

leaving an unpaid bill. And that was the last we heard for a while. There were reports he'd gone bankrupt and had his house repossessed. "He made a fortune," one insider claimed, "and he frittered it away on booze and wild living." By the end of 1994, if reports were true, he was in a rundown flat in north London living off social security. Then there were the first rumours of a comeback. At a party recently he insisted on speaking entirely in dialogue from Spike Lee's *Do The Right Thing*, which offered some hope he'd rediscovered his old maverick touch.

It's a long way back to the old glories but you'd have to be a half-wit to bet against a man of Kev's calibre pulling off a huge comeback. If you need reminding of his genius, slip into those dirty old dungarees, stick your well-worn copy of *Too-Rye-Ay* on the deck and listen in awe... "These people round here wear beaten down eyes/But not us, no not us, we are far too young and clever/ Remember Toora Loora Loora Loo-Rye Aye/Eileen I'll hum this tune forever..."

Yes, yes and yes again.
Jon Wilde

Charlie Watts

October 1998

PEOPLE OFTEN SAY that Mick and Keith are the only Rolling Stones that count. For shame. Look behind Richards (the human riff) and Jagger's scrawny, wiggling arse and there, perched languid and sphinx-like on his stool, is the heart of the band, a man for whom the term dapper could well have been invented: Charlie Watts.

Among the finest and most influential drummers who ever lifted sticks – although, characteristically, he refuses to believe he's any good – he's always detested the non-musical side of being a rock star, keeping a low profile off-stage and stating, "All I really like to do is play the drums with this band. The rest of it I find very difficult to take. The world of rock 'n' roll is a load of crap, all these bloody people, so sycophantic..."

Don't let that fool you, though. "It's Charlie's band," rasps Keith whenever he's asked. "Without him, we wouldn't exist."

Basically speaking, he has been a beacon of unruffled cool for over three decades, a man of style and principle who never moved with the herd. Charlie didn't poke groupies,

wear beads, dally much with class A narcotics or appear in any shit films. He just modestly got on with the job at hand, laying down the beats for the world's greatest rock 'n' roll band, who he has always regarded as nothing more than a group of blokes who get up on stage to play tunes for kids to dance to. Once, when asked what he thought of life as a pop star, he replied: "You live, you die. Even at weekends."

Born on 2 June 1941 in London, the son

Look behind Jagger's scrawny, wiggling arse and there, perched languid and sphinx-like on his stool, is the heart of the band: Charlie Watts.

of a British Rail lorry driver, Charlie started hitting things in his early teens when he took the neck of his newly acquired banjo and began to play it like a drum because the banjo instruction manual looked a bit hard. Eschewing lessons in favour of plenty of practice, he found jazz was his bag, along with imported button-down shirts and Ivy League jackets. At 21 he was playing with Alexis Korner's Blues Incorporated among others, but he never made much bread out of it, once going all the way to Birmingham to perform for just five shillings.

It was around this time that he met the fledgling Stones, and was cajoled into the band shortly before their debut at Soho's Flamingo Club in January 1963. So began a career that has lasted over 35 years to date, not only helping to produce some of the finest rock music one could wish to hear, but also bequeathing a whole stack of sketch books, brimming with the images of every hotel bed he's ever slept in. "It gives you something to do in a hotel room, you know?" he said in the early '80s, and no doubt it kept his mind off the noise Bill Wyman made while sunk to the back wheels in some flighty young piece next door.

After they hit the big time, prancing, preening Jagger

prohibited marriage for the Stones so as not to jeopardise their dangerous sex-bomb image. Charlie was having none of it though, and he eloped in 1965 with his lady, Shirley – to this day still his wife, and without whom on tour he had to be reminded to change his clothes and wash his hair: like as not to emerge later resplendent in cashmere turtle neck, white wool pullover and pearl-grey leather trenchcoat. Ever simple, unaffected and possessing a very dry sense of humour when something tickles him just right, after 30 years of marriage he had this to say about it: "I think the secret of a successful marriage is separate bathrooms."

Although Charlie has often given the impression that he's bored, he says this is not the case, insisting it's just down to the fact that he has an incredibly boring face. He is, however, famously laid-back. While on tour in the States in 1969, he emerged from a restaurant to witness his car being towed away by the LA County Sheriff's department tow truck. Where Keith may have pulled a gun and gone berserk and Mick would have most likely wet his velvet knickers with rage, Charlie could bring himself to utter only, "Oh look, isn't that our car?" as it disappeared before waiting quietly in the shadows until someone did something about it. One can only speculate about his chilled take on towering rage as he sat down for a cup of tea upon discovering he was left off (along with slack-bladder Wyman) the celebrity strewn guest list for Jagger's San Tropez wedding in 1971.

Though he's undoubtedly not one to get his underwear in a knot about trivialities, there is no shortage of starch in Charlie's waistcoat when the occasion demands it. Perhaps the finest single instance of his composure and sense of good taste was the way he dealt with a poncified Jagger in the mid-80s. The band had come together in Amsterdam to discuss future plans and, after a night of carousing with Keith, Mick phoned Charlie's hotel room and woke him. "Is that my drummer? Why don't you get your arse down here," he commanded. Charlie calmly dressed himself in his best

Once, when asked what he thought of life as a pop star, he replied, 'You live, you die. Even at weekends.'

whistle and tie, came down and floored Jagger with a left hook. "Don't ever call me your drummer again," he warned. "You're my fucking singer." A week after this episode Mick offered to forgive Charlie his rash behaviour and the normally docile drummer had to be restrained from smacking him again. Who could blame him?

Now, having slipped into a suitably elegant middle-age some years ago, Charlie plays jazz with his Quintet and mooches about his Devon squire's mansion looking dandy in bow tie, stripped blazer and velvet slippers, listening to the cricket, dusting down his American Civil War memorabilia and

exercising his multitude of dogs. While pounding away laconically behind the Glimmer Twins, eyes shut and mouth pulled up, he has avoided the scandals and controversy that have beset the Stones down the years, shaking his head and shuffling in the opposite direction in his thoughtful, cuticle-chewing hipster slouch. Rising above it all, he's protected the privacy of his family and remained true to what he believed was right – and these days it seems it's Charlie who's the keenest to get down to recording work, having to usher his clapped out cronies through the studio door.

I shall leave the last word to Charlie's singer. On the 1969 live album *Get Your Ya Ya's Out*, between 'Little Queenie' and 'Honkey Tonk Women', Jagger memorably lisps: "Charlie's good tonight, ain't he?" to an almighty cheer. Now there's the thing with Charlie: he's been good every night, looked fantastic while he was at it, and never once let it go to his head. Truly a marvel of a man.
Chas Chandler

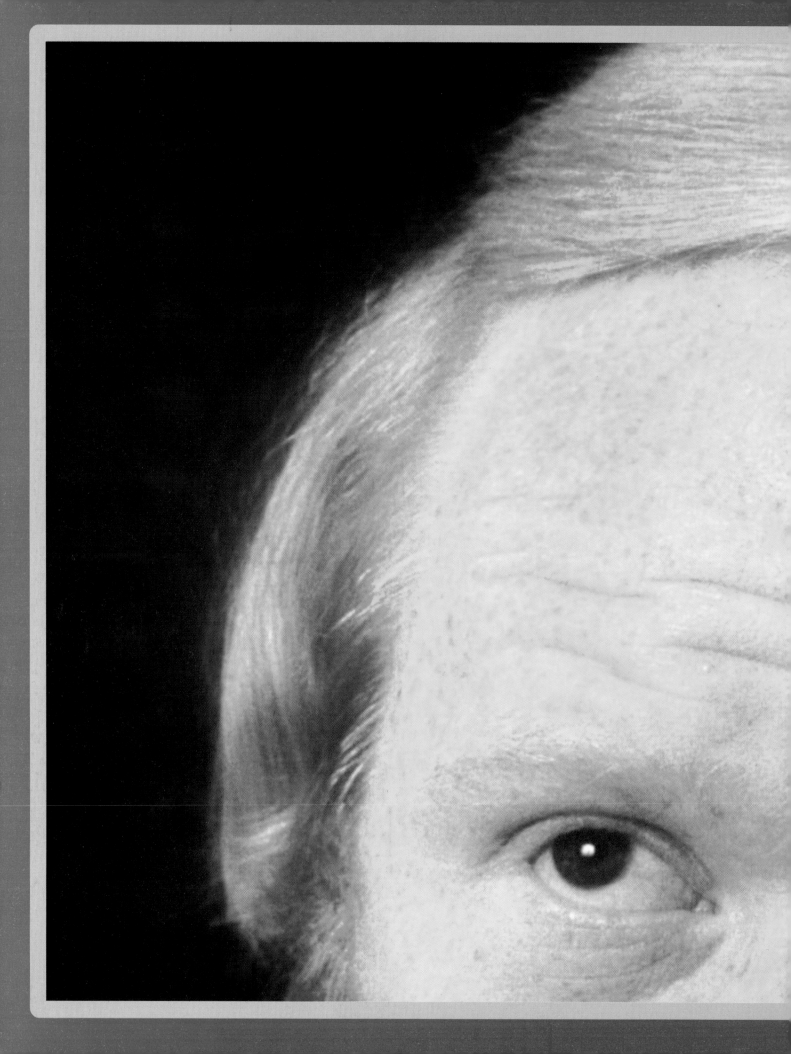

Big Mouths

Jeffrey Bernard

November 1997

COLUMNIST Jeffrey Bernard liked a drink. In fact, he made a career out of it. But he was no ordinary drunk. He worked at it like a golfer works on his handicap. As Soho's most legendary heavy boozer, smoker and self-confessed owner of "the most abused body in London", Jeff Bernard charted and celebrated the destruction of his health like a man picking over the carcass of yesterday's dinner, and was moved to write 700 words a week about it for nearly 20 years.

At the age of 16, he took to Soho like a pissed fish to neat gin, hanging out with hookers and pornographers. He revelled in the lack of discipline, taking jobs as a navvy, a boxer and a gigolo to survive. He took up writing at 31 after being expelled from a naval college for being idle and untrustworthy. At 33, he was told by a doctor that if he had another drink, it would kill him. He spent another 33 years proving him right.

"This is Jeffrey Bernard," said a doctor at the Middlesex hospital, bringing a party of students round to gaze at Jeff's rotting body. "He closes his veins each day with 60 cigarettes, then opens them up again with a bottle of vodka. Tell me, Mr Bernard," said the self righteous quack, "Why do you drink so much?" "To stop myself jogging," sneered Jeff. Unconditional sympathy was the only sort he was interested in and he point blank refused to do anything he didn't want to. Not the easiest way to operate on planet Earth when it comes down to it.

He couldn't give a monkey's tuppence for what anyone

'Why do you drink so much?' 'To stop myself jogging.'

else thought of him. Women, vodka, fighting, failure and accidentally setting light to himself were the staple subjects of his sarky 'Low Life' column in the *Spectator*. He understood none of these things and made this clear. Still, his commitment to being crap at life won him the adoration of millions, and eventually immortalisation as the subject of a play starring Peter O'Toole. Called *Jeffrey Bernard Is Unwell* (a line used by the mag every time he failed to deliver a copy on account of being too arseholed to write it), it was an instant hit much to everyone's surprise, not least his own.

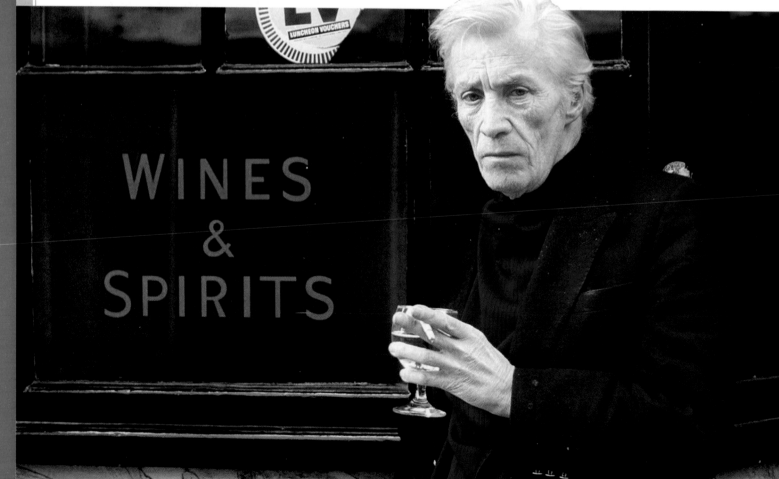

Packed with foul-mouthed stories about the boozing, gambling, arrests, four marriages and financial disasters of some frail, chain-smoking drunk, it ended with the moon coming up over the Coach & Horses (the pub Jeff once described on a hospital release form as his 'next of kin').

I never met the bloke, but everyone I know who did reported quite happily that he was a miserable, bitter and cantankerous old bastard who liked boasting about his love life. When **loaded** was invented, his name cropped up as often as Hunter Thompson's and George Best's, such was the esteem in which berks like ourselves held the poor geezer. We just liked the stories.

A personal favourite was the time he ate a powerful vindaloo, sank a whole bottle of whisky, then went to stay with his friend, the newscaster Sandy Gall, and his wife Eleanor. To his horror, Eleanor served him another curry. That troubled night he woke to find he'd soiled the spare room so seriously he had to sleep on the floor. Shamed, he spent the rest of the day trying to get up the courage to tell Gall's wife. After shuffling up to her four or five times saying, "Er... Eleanor, I... oh, never mind," she finally took pity on him. "It's alright Jeff," she said. "I know. You're in love with me." "Christ, no!" said Jeff, "I've just shat in your son's bed."

His ferocious drinking also made him a legend in the racing world, particularly after the time he threw up a gutful of tomato skins over the Queen Mother while freeloading champagne all day at Ascot.

Inevitably fired from the *Racing Times*, he had little luck seeking employment elsewhere. A brief and unlikely stint under the ex-editor of the *Eagle* comic was, predictably, doomed to failure. The editor, a rather prim ex-vicar, was shocked when a juiced-up Bernard barged into his office demanding some small sum for

Offered a large advance to write his autobiography, he accepted instantly, but produced nothing in return, claiming he'd forgotten everything.

some rubbish he'd written for him. "You cunt, where's my money?" exploded Jeff, catching the former holy man completely off guard – he promptly legged it off to get Jeff's 60 quid. "Thanks a lot," said Jeff, ever the charmer. "I'd have called you a cunt earlier if I'd known that it was the only way to get paid."

Bernard lived in a council flat in a huge tower above Berwick Street market after he had his leg amputated as a result of excessive smoking. Miserable as sin, he tried to make the most of it, placing a personal ad in an upmarket magazine that read: 'Alcoholic geriatric amputee seeks sympathy fuck.' Surprisingly, his track record with women was impressive. He boasted 250 in all, though he later doubled the number when his ex-wife said she didn't think that sounded like very many. Fenella Fielding, the glorious femme fatale of *Carry On Screaming* fame, said he was the wittiest man she'd ever met. Jeff says their ill-fated affair broke up when he fell asleep during sex.

Offered a large advance to write his autobiography, he naturally accepted instantly, but produced nothing in return, claiming he'd forgotten everything. He did put an advert in a local paper asking: "Can anyone tell me what I was doing between 1960 and 1974?" He got one reply: "Yes, you fucked my wife." And after six months, all he'd come up with was 'Reach for the Ground' as a title. Considering it noble-sounding enough, he then called it a day on the project and popped out for another livener.

So, Jeffrey Bernard, or what was left of him, is no more. His timing, as ever, was hopelessly misjudged. Popping his clogs within days of two major scene stealers, he was condemned to hang round St Peter's waiting room with Mother Teresa and Princess Di. Let's hope he took a bottle with him. If they were only taking two out of three that week, he could well have been in trouble: "You're barred Bernard." Oh well, he'll probably get served quicker in the other place.
Mick Bunnage

Brian Clough

April 1997

HEY YOUNG MAN, get your bog head over here and read this. Not many managers manage to combine winning championships and European Cups at unfashionable Midlands clubs with kissing commentators, punching fans and sleeping in a field. But Brian Clough, like his hero Frank Sinatra, did it his way.

Unlike previous great managers such as Sir Matt Busby and Bill Shankly, Clough was prepared to tell the world how good he was. There was the pointing finger, the trademark green jumper and that voice, a memorable know-all nasal whine, always starting with "Weeeeell, David..." In the early '70s even Muhammad Ali was moved to ask, "Who is this guy Clough?"

At Derby, the young Clough declared: "I am conceited in having taken a side like Derby, worked bloody hard and got them to where we are now. I think conceit and arrogance are part of a man's make-up."

As a player he was a formidable striker with Middlesbrough and Sunderland but won only two England caps. After retiring early due to injury, the young Clough took over at Hartlepool and then Derby, where he turned journeymen pros like John McGovern and John O'Hara into stars and won the second division in 1968-69 and the League Championship in 1971-72. Yet despite this success the directors disliked Clough's media profile. The end came after a win at Old Trafford. A Derby director beckoned Peter Taylor with his finger and Cloughie decided it was a bunch of arse: "I told the board they could stick their four year contract up their jacksie."

A spell at Brighton followed and then a 44-day stint at Leeds. At Derby Clough had been critical of Don Revie's side and the players resented him from the off. The board queried his attempt to buy Peter Shilton, panicked and sacked him.

Clough was presented with a cheque for £25,000 by Leeds chairman Manny Cousins and drove to London to make sure it cleared: "I didn't trust them at all," was Cloughie's reasoning behind the jaunt.

But Clough came back and he and Taylor joined Nottingham Forest, bottom of the second division, in 1975. They signed Shilton, turned Coventry reserve Larry Lloyd and wild man Kenny Burns into an impregnable defence and watched players like John Robertson develop. "People thought he couldn't play. But get good players around him and he blossomed. It was like giving him a shovel full of manure." Clough continued to shovel the manure and the result was promotion, the League Championship in 1977-78, two League Cups and two European Cups in 1978-79 and 1979-80. Contrary to popular belief, Clough didn't rule through fear – his main ability was helping the players relax, famously insisting they all had a few beers on the eve of a League Cup Final.

In 1977 he was interviewed for the England manager's job. His biggest mistake was upsetting the FA's Ted Croker by saying he'd scrap England's poncy Admiral shirts: "He said, 'We've got to move with the times.' I said, 'Bullshit, a Rolls Royce is a Rolls Royce and white is good for England.'" Clough didn't get the job.

Clough lost his way a little at Forest in the early '80s, mainly through signing duff strikers like Justin Fashanu, Ian Wallace and Peter Ward. Clough had his suspicions about the then still in the closet Fashanu and summoned him to his office for a memorable confrontation.

"Where do you go if you want to buy a loaf of bread?" asked Cloughie.

'I think conceit and arrogance are part of a man's make-up.'

"A baker's, I suppose," said Fashanu.

"Where do you go for a leg of lamb?"

"A butcher's," replied the non-scoring centre forward.

"So why do you keep going to that bloody poofs' club in town?" inquired Clough.

There was still the TV work and the highlight of Cloughie's punditry came during the 1986 World Cup. Faced with yokel hero Mike Channon exclaiming, "We've got to get bodies in the box, the French do it! The Danes do it! The Brazilians do it!" Cloughie replied deadpan, "Yes, and even educated bees do it."

By the end of the '80s Clough, now without Taylor but aided by 'the number nine', his son Nigel, was back on form. Forest won the League Cup in 1989 and 1990 and reached the FA Cup Final 1991. His motivational tactics remained as unusual as ever. In his autobiography Lee Chapman recalled how at half-time

Clough told Nigel Jemson to stand up and asked, "Young man have you ever been punched in the stomach?"

"As soon as Nigel said 'No', a forceful blow was delivered to his midriff." revealed Chappy. "Nigel doubled up in

pain. 'Now you have, son,' said Clough and turned away."

Cloughie's behaviour was becoming more erratic. He was fined by the FA for punching pitch invaders after a League Cup tie and then photographed kissing them and making up. Allegations of his drinking were whispered and indeed, anyone who kisses ITV's Gary Newbon must surely have been on the sauce.

During the 1992-93 season *The Sunday Mirror* reported that Clough had been found in a ditch by a local fireman. Clough countered in the *Sun* that he often slept in fields. "I had a kip in a field because I

was tired." Sadly Clough stayed a season too long, Forest were relegated and he retired with an emotional send-off from the fans.

In 1994 Clough admitted in his autobiography "I have drunk too much for my own good on occasions," and that he had listened to his friends and family and was off the booze.

Thankfully Old Big 'Ead recently checked out of a health clinic and attended a Forest match against Coventry to see young Nigel play. The game needs him. Cloughie is still loved by the fans for his plain speaking and his teams who never argued with refs and played proper football. As he once said: "If God had meant football to be played in the air, he'd have put grass in the sky." Brian Clough: top young man.

Pete May

Tony Gubba

September 2000

SO WHAT NOW for Gubba? What happens to the least charismatic man in football when the final whistle blows on *MOTD* next spring? A call from Des, anxious to add some beef to ITV's flashy but powder-puff midfield? Sharp-suited lunches with the big boys at Sky, ready to pay over the odds for the cool authority that only a bald Lancastrian can bring? Or will he simply make do with whatever scraps of underwater badminton and floodlit monkey wrestling the Beeb can find to keep him going until he retires?

It's not been, in the traditional sense, a brilliant career. But that's exactly how Tony's paymasters wanted it from the start – from the day, 27 years ago, that this unknown 29-year-old newshound

The boy Gubba was perfect, partly because his personality wasn't capable of taking over a rabbit warren.

was unveiled as the new face of *Sportsnight*. David Coleman's departure had been something of a shock, and BBC Sport wanted a solid, reliable replacement whose personality wouldn't threaten to take over the show. The boy Gubba was perfect, partly because his personality wasn't capable of taking over a rabbit warren. And he's played the same loyal role ever since: slotting in, mopping up and not swearing or hitting anyone on live television.

Not that he gets much live work, of course. Even in Euro 2000, Gubba was the highlights man. While Motty bumbled more idiotically than ever before, and Barry spouted more pompously than ever before, Tony turned up on the graveyard shift to say "Ohhhhhh, yes!" whenever someone scored. Hardly inspired, but as countless managers must have told him over the years, you need someone like that in your team.

He's not your man for Colemanballs either. Gubbsy knows how to warp logic in that special way they only teach at commentating

school, but he isn't there to be laughed at. Crediting Dennis Bergkamp with laying on "75 percent of Arsenal's nine goals" (I make that an impressive 6.75) is about as daft as he gets, unless you count one faintly sinister observation that "the ball must be as slippery as a wet baby". I've never kicked a wet baby myself, but you have to admit the poetry of it.

There have been other achievements too. He wrote a sports quiz book in 1978. Ten years later after that (it's best to pace yourself), he supplied commentary for the computer game *International Superstar Soccer '98*. Who knows? In 2008 he might build an award-winning rockery or invent a new kind of pencil.

By then, I suppose, all commentators will be like Jonathan Pearce. So perhaps it's as well Tony has the chance to hang up his microphone with dignity now. He is a gentlemen and a pro. If he'd only had a slightly less weedy voice and a sharper eye for the telling final ball, he could have been right up there. Ohhhh yes.

Richard Purvis

While Motty bumbled more idiotically than ever before, Tony turned up on the graveyard shift to say 'Ohhhhhh, yes!' whenever someone scored.

Jesus

January 1999

HARK THE HERALD Angels sing! The Lord Jesus is born! No crib for a bed! Surrounded by donkeys and geese! Worshipped by lowly shepherds, pearly kings, David Bowie and Sting. Behold His wonder, lying there all pink and lovely, the King of Kings, born under a star. Just like Lee Marvin.

Yep, Jesus is quite literally THE Greatest Living Englishman to ever draw breath or punch someone outside a chip shop. Don't be taken in by that laughable old-wives tale that Jesus was born in a stable in Bethlehem. Have you ever seen a picture of Jesus? Does he have a crumb-

Don't be taken in by that laughable old-wives tale that Jesus was born in a stable in Bethlehem. Have you ever seen a picture of Jesus? Does the Son of God look like a suicide bomber?

strewn moustache and an AK-47? Does the Son of God look like a suicide bomber? Of course not. He's a strapping blue-eyed prop-forward with a Goth-white complexion and 'Love' tattooed across both knuckles. Jesus is as English as peas.

Sure, it's easy to be taken in by those Ladybird book pictures of Jesus lugging crosses about in a dressing gown. But that was just the year he worked on a Kibbutz. No, Jesus was actually from Macclesfield. Mr and Mrs Christ had that big bungalow over on Grisedale Way. Lovely couple. Jewish, I believe.

Think about it: Jesus' *real* dad is an Englishman. Whenever God's on the telly, He has James Mason's voice, Richard Harris' beard and Eric Morecambe's overcoat. QED, the Son of God is made from pies like the rest of us.

I'm convinced this 'Bethlehem' thing is a huge conspiracy by an Israeli tourist board desperate to off-load a job-lot of

'I've Been to Christ's House' commemorative combs.

If Jesus really had grown up in Galilee – a violent police state occupied by nasty Romans – he would have spent all day chucking rocks at soldiers and collecting prosthetic limbs. But Jesus spent his youth dicking about down the shops being tempted by the Devil like everyone else. Although, personally, I never had a fisherman friend called 'Simon'.

If so-called 'Christians' like Roy Castle and Gloria Hunniford really expect us to believe *The Bible's* version of the story, they'll have to patch up a few glaring holes in the plot. Take Luke 1:31:

"An angel appeared unto Mary and said, 'Rejoice for you will be with child!'

'How will this be,' Mary asked the angel, 'since I am a virgin?' The angel answered, 'Don't be afraid, for The Holy Spirit will come on you.'"

Ugh. Filthy. That's the sort of hideous contraception mistake Claire Raynor is forever mopping up. But there was worse to come back at Joseph's shed.

Mary: "Umm, Joey love? I don't know how to tell you this, but I'm up the duff."

Joseph: "WHAT?"

Mary: "'Fraid so. I did one of them kits from Boots."

Joseph: "WHAT?"

Mary: "But it's OK. God reckons it was him."

Joseph: "WHAT?"

Mary: "Yeah, I know! The sly old fox, eh?"

Predictably unconvinced by this fairy tale, Joseph goes mental. Fearing for the Holy Foetus, God sends an angel to Joseph and says,

"Joseph, do not be afraid to take Mary home as your wife, because what is conceived in her is from the Holy Spirit." (Matthew 1:20)

His argument being that if you have it away with James Mason in a phonebox after a half of Campari, it's OK because he's famous. Peter Stringfellow uses the same technique, I believe. And jelly-spined Joseph swallows it all like Ian Beale:

"It may not be me own child, Pat, but vat child needs larve! 'Ow can I frow 'im art inter ver cold?" (EastEnders 3:16)

Distressed by this crap plot-twist, Mary immediately goes into labour and pops the Messiah out in a stable crammed with livestock and gaping tourists.

Now, the Nativity is a British tradition if ever there was one. In fact, I vividly remember Jesus being involved when I played 'Third Shepherd' in the 1976 Ivy

Of course, traditionalists will insist that Jesus was a foreigner and that Christmas is all about an event staged behind a pub 2000 years ago. That's just selfish talk.

Bank Primary production. And it was quite a wooden performance from the Lamb of God, if I remember rightly. He just sat there in the papier mache manger they'd knocked up in Mrs Bagley's art class. In fact, I never realised until now; I must have gone to school with Jesus! I always wondered why that weirdo in the sandals was excused from RE and woodwork.

Of course, traditionalists – the blind fools! – will insist that Jesus was a foreigner and that Christmas is all about an event staged behind a pub 2000 years ago. That's just selfish talk. As Sir Harry Secombe will tell you, Jesus is Everywhere, He is the Way and the

Light, and He sees Everything, particularly when you're trying on your sister's pants. Jesus is, in a very real sense, Living In All Of Us. Apart from the French.

And this is why the English, being a benevolent race, invented Christmas. We thought the savage heathens elsewhere in the Empire would benefit from the Great British Christ-related traditions of Mary Poppins, sprouts, Hai-Karate, Scalextric, gloom and depression. God Bless us one and all.

But, as we're tucking into our mince pies and drunkenly pawing Deirdre from number six, we should never lose sight of the true meaning of Christmas: an innocent little baby, free from sin, gurgling and burping, naked and pink on a bed of straw. And you killed him. Merry Christmas.

John Perry

The Newspaper Vendor

March 1999

SOME MEN are born great. Some men achieve greatness. Some men have greatness thrust upon them. And some men wouldn't know greatness if it ripped their head off and pissed essence of greatness in the seeping hole.

But there is one man who is all of those four categories and more. He is a man without a name, or even a number. He is a man you meet every day, in every

He is the Godfather of Good News, The Man Who Shouts Incoherently At Every News Stand In Britain.

town, and yet a man whose face you would never remember. He is a man who would ask you no questions, tell you no lies and request no quarter beyond, erm,

maybe something smaller than a fiver, because he only keeps a small float, see and he can't change that, guv. Unless you want it in 20ps? He is the Godfather of Good News, the Capo di Tutti Capo of Communication. He is The Man Who Shouts Incoherently At Every News Stand In Britain.

Everything about him is shrouded in mystery. Where did he come from? How did he get his job? Who is the mysterious 13-year-old Roland Browning lookalike and mute bag lady standing either side of him? And why is he unable to speak properly? Let us attempt to explain.

You know this man. He's the one standing behind that strange metal box with a pile of newspapers shouting. At first he might appear to be merely grunting. But listen carefully and you can decipher a distant trace of English. When he shouts "Suuyyyy fayyyyyyy!", for example, he means "City Final". Likewise,

Some men wouldn't know greatness even if it ripped their head off and pissed essence of greatness in the seeping hole.

"Ayyyee Stuuuygh" is a derivation of "Evening Standard". Listen to your local news warrior, and you can no doubt fill in your own regional version.

Now, at first glance, he may appear a bit simple, barely human even. But this is a short-sighted view. He simply practises economy of language. No extravagant sales pitch, no flowery patter, why use three syllables when one will do? We could all learn something from that.

In a world cruelly shorn of romance, he is a Dickensian throwback to an age of good, honest media values, when the news was news, and these stout public servants were the proud messengers of the information superdirt-track. OK, so over the years they forgot how to tell anyone about it in comprehensible English, but by that time they didn't need to say anything, simply make a noise, like a human news siren. Who needs words when you've got a foghorn and the truth?

This is a man that all right-thinking people must admire. Imagine the gyp this poor bastard has put up with down the years. Consider, if you will, how a mind can be numbed beyond recognition by a million people going "Oops, I'm throwing it away! Ha-hur!" when they drop a coin. Imagine having to make ten-second conversations about how "Brrrrr! It's a bit

fresh today, eh?" every half a minute. Any ordinary reasonable human being would soon crack under the sheer pressure of dullness, take out an Uzi, shout "Valhalla! I am coming!" and mow down an entire pedestrian precinct.

But even if you think you are man enough for this unenviable working environment, don't even think about going to your local careers adviser and asking them about your prospects. It's a closed shop.

For starters, you're already too old. You know the 10-year-olds in shorts and flat caps who shout "Read all about it!" in old films about Victorian England? Well they're still doing it now, only they're at least 100 years old.

Besides, it's who you know. For the last 300 years, the industry has been ruled by shady dynasties. Since the late '70s, the leading news-stand families have been the Hnyuuuuyghs and the Myesyuuuuys. They carved up the country in the wake of the infamous 'Ink Wars' of 1977, when industrial action by the print unions during the Winter of Discontent opened the way for sabotage on a scale approaching raw anarchy. The Liverpool based Yeeauuuuuygh's, for example, supplied false newspapers for the unwitting vendors of rival families, filled with pictures of animals wanking, and rogue headline sheets such as "No news, piss off" to discourage their thousands of customers.

In a spectacular revenge attack involving an arsenal of sharpened 10p pieces (the old, lethal, fit between the knuckle types) and some tanks, the entire Yeeauuuuuygh family were brutally liquidated, and legend has it that one famous sports pink was coloured entirely with their blood.

But there's an even stronger social subtext at work here. Experts believe the news vendor's distinctive dribbling demeanour, snorting and nervous twitches are the result of centuries of careful inbreeding. See the woman and the boy standing next to him? They're his wife, daughter, brother-in-law and son.

OK, they may look odd to you with

your fancy modern ways but don't you dare take the piss, pal. Many vendors can decapitate a victim with a sharply folded first edition, Odd-Job like, at distances of up to 100 yards.

This man is indestructible, unsackable and unflappable. If the paper's headline said "IT'S ARMAGEDDON!! FOUR MINUTE WARNING STARTED THREE MINUTES AGO!!" he would not flee, flounder or fret. He would stand tall, proud and strong. And probably absorb the fucking blast.

After all, he has survived being on the front line for all the greatest social upheavals of our time: war, famine, the introduction of 'fiddly' ™ five pence pieces... and some say there are newspaper sellers around who remember the revolutionary switch from groats to shillings in 1581.

In an age of uncertainty and moral turpitude, somehow you know that this, this *icon* of truth, justice and the British way will survive long into the next millennium and beyond.

So next time you go to buy a paper, doff your cap, offer a cheery greeting, in gibberish if you wish, and pay your respects. Bow down at his news altar – because truly, we are not wuuuuuuuy.

Johnny Sharp

Sid Waddell

January 1995

'When Alexander of Macedonia was 33 he cried salt tears because there were no more worlds to conquer. Eric Bristow is only 27!' The man's a poet.

"*D*ENNIS OVENS has goosed the cook.*" My favourite story about legendary Geordie darts commentator Sid Waddell happened during a live television game. Sid's heart was pumping hard as the game neared its climax and he dipped into his vast reservoir of uncanny phrases, declaring:

"*It couldn' t be more exciting if Elvis Presley walked in and asked for a bag of chips!*"

As the puzzled TV audience tried to make some sense of it all, Sid felt something weird himself, a slippery tickle on his lips followed by the sight of two orange objects swimming in front of his eyes. "I thought I'd gone insane," he recalls, "then I realised I was so entranced in the game I hadn't noticed some bugger had slipped two goldfish into me glass of water! On live TV! Didn't stop laughing for a week."

"*And the chips are in the fat.*"

Sid Waddell has been mesmerising darts fans for years with his breathless, bizarre and infectiously passionate commentating style. Who else could get away with advising the nation that the two fellows on the ocke were like a couple of scientists sending a ballistic missile continent to continent?

"*Jocky Wilson – all the psychology of a claymore.*"

Born in Newcastle and raised on a diet of dominoes and chips, Sid was quite a scholar, graduating from Cambridge where he got darts made into a blue ribbon event before suffering his worst ever darts moment – losing to a team of vicars in his local pub. After college, he moved into television and in the early '70s, managed to get *Indoor League*, which included darts, women arm wrestling and skittles, put on the box.

"And Bobby George is sweating like a swamp donkey."

He wrote the captivating children's TV classic *Jossie's Giants* about a junior Geordie football team with a penchant for *Scooby Doo* type capers. The show attracted seven million viewers. Recently he penned BBC1's successful *Sloggers* series which is basically *Jossie's Giants* except it's about a cricket team.

"This lad's into computers – he's a pelican chip off the old block."

Sid's TV darts career started in 1977 with David Vine on a Chorley balcony. Before long the BBC had to make him a special soundproof commentary box. "I'm one of the loudest in the world," he boasts, "I can strip paint." By 1980 he was as popular and important amongst the darts fraternity as any of the players.

"He walked in like the Laughing Cavalier and he's leaving looking like Lee Van Cleef."

Sid has never pulled his punches. If he thinks Jocky Wilson is playing like a berk, he'll say so and the players actually respect him for his honesty.

"He's snapping at his heels like an alligator with toothache."

Imagine John Motson confronting Alex Ferguson following a bad Man Utd defeat and scoffing: "You lot were garbage, Alex. Cantona was crap and your "keeper prances like a ponce." It just wouldn't happen.

'It couldn't be more exciting if Elvis Presley walked in and asked for a bag of chips!'

"Three 140s on the trot – and the last one was 100."

"You see darts is so accessible compared to other sports," Sid once told me. "You could be in a pub in Leeds and end up playing darts with Eric Bristow if he's in town but when was the last time you saw Bjorn Borg down Pudsey social club?"

"The atmosphere in here is a cross between the Munich Beer Festival and the Colosseum at Rome... with the Christians on the menu."

You could be forgiven for thinking that

Sid is just plain bonkers. He's said a lot of weird stuff (which has made him a regular in *Private Eye's* Colemanballs column) while doing the BBC's coverage of the World Championships over the years and he's repeating it now on Sky who, much to Sid's glee, screen several darts tournaments each year.

"This kid is a real hard practiser. He's been burning the midnight oil at both ends."

"I remember.one time when I had gout in me right knee. I was in the box with me leg in bandages and I had this nervous cough which I'd conceal by muffling the microphone in a big piece of rubber foam strapped to me right arm. I was in there and I got all excited and stood up like this mad Egyptian mummy and, forgetting me leg was all strapped up I swung it round and knocked the commentary door clear off its hinges and down the stairs live on air. It made a right racket."

"When Alexander of Macedonia was 33 he cried salt tears because there were no more worlds to conquer. Eric Bristow is only 27!"

The man's a poet.
Tim Southwell

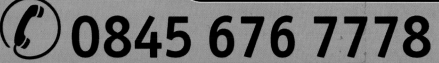